OSPREY AIRCRAFT OF THE ACES • 27

Typhoon and Tempest Aces of World War 2

SERIES EDITOR: TONY HOLMES

OSPREY AIRCRAFT OF THE ACES • 27

Typhoon and Tempest Aces of World War 2

Chris Thomas

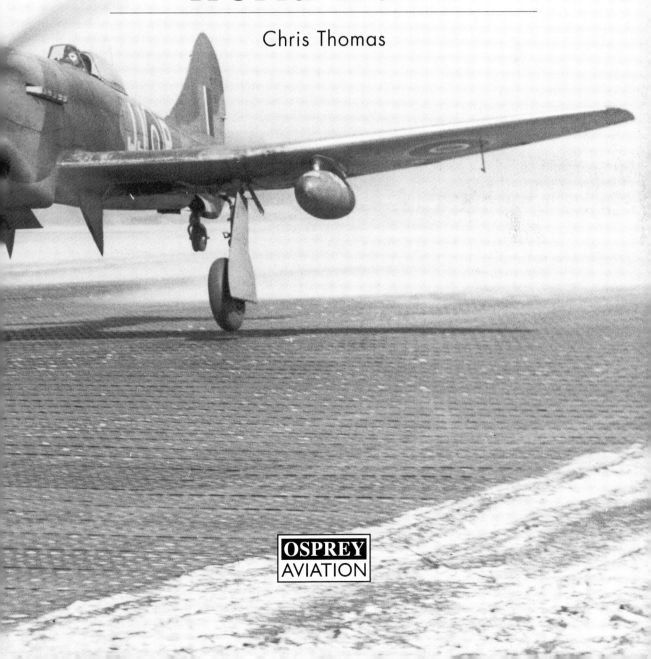

OSPREY
AVIATION

Front cover
On 12 March 1943, Flt Sgt 'Pinkie' Stark of No 609 Sqn was flying between North and South Foreland, off the Kent coast, on an 'anti-Rhubarb' patrol with Sgt Leslie. At 1015 hours, they received information from Hornchurch that 'two-plus bandits were proceeding in an easterly direction, ten miles north-east of Calais'. After various manoeuvres over the Channel, four Fw 190s were sighted and the No 609 Sqn pair managed to position themselves behind two of the enemy aircraft. Stark's combat report continues;

'I attacked the leading machine, opening fire at 100 yards from astern. I saw strikes on the fuselage and starboard wing. Several objects fell off the aircraft, and flames appeared round the cockpit. Quite a large area appeared to be flaming. He turned to port slowly and I pulled up to avoid collision. Turning steeply to port and looking down, I saw the enemy aircraft going down in a 30° dive, almost on his back.'

This was Stark's first air combat success, and he would go on to be credited with five more enemy aircraft destroyed in the air and finish the war as No 609 Sqn's commanding officer. His victim was Feldwebel Emil Boesch, flying 'Black 12' (Wk-Nr 0829) of 10(*Jabo*)./JG 54 – one of 42 Fw 190s to fall to the guns of the Typhoon during the campaign against the Luftwaffe fighter-bombers.

'Pinkie' Stark was flying DN406 'PR-F' on this occasion, which became the subject of a well-known series of photographs taken at Manston a few weeks later. The scoreboard above the aircraft's wing root recorded locomotives destroyed on night intruders over occupied France and Belgium (*cover artwork by Iain Wyllie*)

For a Catalogue of all books published by Osprey Aviation, Military and Automotive please write to:

The Marketing Manager, Osprey Publishing Ltd., P.O. Box 140, Wellingborough, Northants NN8 4ZA, United Kingdom
E-mail: info@OspreyDirect.co.uk

Osprey Direct USA, P.O. Box 130, Sterling Heights, MI 48311-0130, USA
E-mail: info@OspreyDirectUSA.com

OR VISIT THE OSPREY WEBSITE AT:
http://www.osprey-publishing.co.uk

First published in Great Britain in 1999
by Osprey Publishing, Elms Court, Chapel Way
Botley, Oxford, OX2 9LP

ISBN 1 85532 779 1

Edited by Tony Holmes
Page design by TT Designs, T & B Truscott
Cover Artwork by Iain Wyllie
Aircraft Profiles by Chris Davey
Figure Artwork by Mike Chappell
Scale Drawings by Mark Styling
Origination by Grasmere Digital Imaging, Leeds, UK
Printed through Bookbuilders, Hong Kong

99 00 01 02 03   10 9 8 7 6 5 4 3 2 1

ACKNOWLEDGEMENTS
A wide network of Typhoon and Tempest pilots and groundcrew, enthusiasts and fellow researchers have helped me compile the records which support this publication. To them, I wish to express my thanks once again. I would particularly like to acknowledge the help of the following individuals; James and Michael Baldwin (sons of the late Grp Capt J R Baldwin), Wg Cdr R P Beamont, the late Hugh Fraser, Lt Col R A Lallemant, the late Sqn Ldr F Murphy, the late Grp Capt D J Scott, Sqn Ldr C J Sheddan and Sqn Ldr L W F Stark.

Thank you also to Christopher Shores, my co-author on *The Typhoon and Tempest Story*, and, with Clive Williams, author of the seminal *Aces High*, from which I have, with permission, freely drawn information. Norman Franks also helped out with photos and extracts from some of his authoritative works (see the bibliography). Finally, thanks to Paul Sortehaug for supplying photos and extracts from *Wild Winds*, his recently published comprehensive history of No 486 Sqn, which is the result of many years dedicated research (copies are available from the author at 4 William Street, Dunedin, New Zealand).

EDITOR'S NOTE
To make this best-selling series as authoritative as possible, the editor would be interested in hearing from any individual who may have relevant photographs, documentation or first-hand experiences relating to the elite pilots, and their aircraft, of the various theatres of war. Any material used will be fully credited to its original source. Please write to Tony Holmes at 10 Prospect Road, Sevenoaks, Kent, TN13 3UA, Great Britain.

CONTENTS

INTRODUCTION

Hawker Typhoon and Tempest - two aircraft types with widely differing reputations. The former was a technical nightmare redeemed as a ground attack machine, whilst the latter proved to be the most superlative low and medium level fighter to see service with the RAF, and arguably any air force, during the latter stages of World War 2. Yet what of their air combat successes? Strange to relate, both types were credited with almost identical totals of enemy aircraft destroyed in the air – 246 by the Typhoon and 239 by the Tempest. The success of both aircraft in the pure fighter role was restricted not so much by their technical limitations (although problems of this nature did have some bearing on the Typhoon in its early service career), but by the circumstances of the air war during their respective periods of service.

By the time the Typhoon was in widespread use, it was largely restricted to a defensive role as the most effective counter to marauding Luftwaffe fighter-bombers that threatened English coastal towns. A brief period of spectacular success on offensive operations followed, especially when long-range tanks became available, but it was not long before the Typhoon force was absorbed into the 2nd Tactical Air Force (2nd TAF). As D-Day approached, the Typhoon squadrons were all equipped with rockets or bombs and dedicated to the close support and interdiction roles, which gave limited opportunity for air combat.

When the Tempest entered service, its air combat potential was enormous. However, its entry into this field was delayed, perversely, by the aircraft's own excellence, for soon after its first aerial successes, it was withdrawn from the Normandy air war to spearhead defences against the V1. A full three months would pass before the first Tempest Wing was able to join the rest of the 2nd TAF fighter squadrons on the Continent. Having missed the D-Day air battles, with their rich pickings for the 2nd TAF Spitfire and Mustang Wings, the Tempest units were left with just six months of action against determined, but dwindling, Luftwaffe forces.

Against this background it can be seen that Typhoon and Tempest pilots had little opportunity to build up big scores. The relative few who become 'aces' by the traditional reckoning did so by seizing their limited chances, and sometimes by going out and making them. It has to be said that there were many pilots who were just as capable, including some with already impressive scores, who were not able to claim any air-to-air victories whilst flying these types. Among them were superbly skilled, aggressive and highly motivated leaders who would develop the art of ground attack to new heights, setting the standards for years to come. While this book celebrates the top-scoring aerial aces, I would not wish their less high-profile comrades to be forgotten.

Author's note
The text of this book is interspersed with many quotes from original combat reports, and these have been reproduced verbatim, with original spellings, abbreviations and grammar, which do not follow the conventions used in the rest of the text.

INTO SERVICE AND OUT?

9August 1942. Two dark grey-green shapes flit across the North Sea, 50 miles off Cromer, on the Norfolk coast. One is at barely 50 ft, the other at 800 ft above the sea. They are Hawker Typhoons of No 266 'Rhodesia' Sqn - only the second frontline unit to fly Fighter Command's newest, most advanced and most troublesome fighter aircraft. The pilots, Plt Offs I M Munro and N J Lucas, scan the horizon in the hope of detecting Luftwaffe reconnaissance aircraft.

Suddenly, an aircraft is seen at 2 o'clock, zero feet and one mile distant, but closing rapidly. Too late to take avoiding action, the aircraft passes beneath the Section and is identified as a Ju 88. The Typhoons turn hard in opposite directions and surge forward as the throttles are opened. With more than 2000 horsepower driving each Typhoon, and the ASI needles winding round towards '360 indicated', the chase is soon over.

Munro attacks from astern, whilst Lucas peels off to port and attacks from that quarter. Both Typhoons open fire at 600 yards, closing to 200 before breaking off their attacks. Under the combined fire from the four Hispano 20 mm cannon carried by Munro's Typhoon and the 12 0.303-in machine guns of Lucas's aircraft, the Ju 88 bursts into flames and crashes into the sea. The first kill for the Hawker Typhoon, and the first of many for this lethal combination of horsepower and fire power . . . but it had been a long time coming.

To understand how this situation had come about, it is necessary to return to the origins of the Typhoon. With the Hawker Hurricane barely

One of only two photos showing an example of No 56 Sqn's initial Typhoon IA equipment (with original opaque cockpit fairing) to have come to light. No 'official' photos seem to have been taken, and security would have been tight round the 'top secret' newcomer, especially at Duxford, home of the Air Fighting Development Unit. Note the canvas doped over the six machine-gun ports in each wing. On the original print a faint 'B' can be seen on the leading edge, suggesting that this may be R7594 'US-B' (*PAC*)

Commanding No 56 Sqn for most of its first year with Typhoons was Sqn Ldr Hugh 'Cocky' Dundas. Combat victories would elude Dundas during this fraught year, but he already had a string of successes gained in 1940/41 with No 616 Sqn, and would later add more when leading No 324 Wing in the Mediterranean. His final tally was four and six shared destroyed, two shared probables and two and one shared damaged (*via N Franks*)

The second unit to receive the troublesome new fighter was No 266 (Rhodesia) Sqn, commanded by Sqn Ldr Charles Green, seen here in the cockpit of his personal Typhoon 'ZH-G' (R7686 to September 1942, R7915 to February 1943 and EJ924 to July 1943). When he left the unit, he wrote in his log book 'what a marvellous kite' (*IWM CH 18164*)

in production, Hawker's Chief Designer, Sidney Camm, directed his thoughts towards a successor. Rather than a step by step development of the Hurricane, an ambitious leap forward using untried technology was proposed. It was intended that the new design would utilise one of the 2000 hp engines then under development, and traditional wood and fabric structure would be abandoned in favour of an all-metal design.

In January 1937 the Air Ministry issued specification F.18/37, which called for the development of an advanced fighter aircraft to eventually replace the Spitfire and Hurricane. Its outstanding requirement was that the new aircraft should have the greatest possible speed margin over the contemporary bomber. Indeed, the successful contender was expected to have a top speed in excess of 400 mph at 15,000 ft. Armament was to be 'not less than 12 Browning guns (0.303-in), and the aircraft must be a steady platform for them at its maximum speed'.

Camm designed two variants of his new type, one featuring a Rolls-Royce engine which would eventually be named the Vulture, and the other utilising a Napier engine which duly became the Sabre. Construction of prototypes of each design began in March 1938 and, following Hawker's established 'wind' theme, they were named Tornado and Typhoon respectively.

The Hurricane was large compared with other fighters of the time, but these aircraft nearly doubled the loaded weight of their predecessor, weighing in at around 11,000 lbs as opposed to 6500 lbs. The Tornado flew first, in December 1939, and the Typhoon some three months later. Test flying and development continued throughout the spring of 1940, but was hindered by the Battle of Britain, when the aviation industry's priorities were to maximise production of existing types.

The first production Typhoon did not fly until 27 May 1941, and the first (and only) production Tornado took to the air the following August. Terminal problems with the latter's Vulture engine led to the abandonment of any further development, however, and resulted in the cancellation of Tornado production.

Meanwhile, Typhoons were rolling off the production line at Gloster Aircraft, the first four going for trials at A&AEE and RAE and the next two to the Air Fighting Development Unit (AFDU) for brief tactical evaluation. Comparative tests against the Spitfire V showed the Typhoon to be 40 mph faster at all levels above 14,000 ft, and even faster below that level. The heavyweight Typhoon was, of course, less manoeuvrable than the Spitfire, but the AFDU concluded that it would be possible to utilise the Typhoon's high-speed to good advantage.

Despite a number of the outstanding modifications necessary to turn the aircraft into a fighting machine, and the known unreliability of the complex Sabre engine, Fighter Command decided to equip a squadron with the new type. The

unit chosen was No 56 Sqn, then based at Duxford flying Hurricane Mk IIBs. The commanding officer, Sqn Leader Prosser Hanks, had achieved 'ace' status early in the Battle of France (see *Osprey Aircraft of the Aces 18 - Hurricane Aces 1939-40* for further details), adding to his score while instructing at Aston Down during the Battle of Britain and later with No 257 Sqn – his score then stood at nine destroyed and a shared probable. The first Typhoon IAs arrived in September, and by the end of October 1941, the unit had a full complement.

The arrival of the first Typhoons came at a time of great reorganisation within Fighter Command, and shortly before Christmas 1941 a new commanding officer arrived on the squadron. Newly-promoted Sqn Ldr 'Cocky' Dundas was to take over from Prosser Hanks, who in turn was also promoted to take over the Duxford Wing. This would be a short term appointment for Hanks, for in February 1942 he would move to Coltishall, and then a few months later to Malta to command the Luqa Wing (where he increased his final score to 13 destroyed, 1 and 3 shared probable and 6 damaged).

In addition to inheriting the technical maladies then associated with the Typhoon, Dundas also had a more personal problem – a broken leg, which had been the result of a game off 'mess rugger'. His autobiography *Flying Start* reveals the extent of his problems on taking over;

'I soon discovered that enthusiasm for the Typhoons was lukewarm, to say the least. The first of these new planes had been delivered in September, and since then there had been nothing but trouble. On 1 November there had been a fatal accident, when an officer of the squadron had unaccountably dived straight into the ground in a Typhoon from a height of 3000 ft. It was later discovered that he had been poisoned by carbon monoxide, and all Typhoons were immediately grounded. By the time I reached the squadron on 22 December, a small number had been modified and passed fit for flying. Meanwhile, the squadron had to maintain a state of readiness with its few remaining Hurricanes – a tedious and unrewarding business unlikely to yield any results in the form of contact with the enemy.

'Having at last disposed of my plaster cast, I made my first flight in the Typhoon on 2 January 1942. Taxying out, I felt as though I was about to try to take off in a steam roller. But once off the ground, I soon responded to the sense of excitement engendered by the plane's speed and power. I did a couple of rolls over the airfield and came in for a careful and landing.

'My pilots crowded round to get my first reactions. What did I think of her? "I think she's great", I said. "The speed is really exciting. And what a steady gun platform she must make. But one thing's certain. We're not going to war until the rear view is improved. That will have to be put right".'

While a canopy modification was

Completing the Duxford Typhoon Wing was No 609 Sqn, whose CO was Sqn Ldr Paul Richey, author of that early war classic *Fighter Pilot*. Like Dundas, he had no opportunity to add to his score (ten and one shared destroyed, one unconfirmed destroyed, one and one shared probable and six damaged), but would play a key role in coaxing the Typhoon into its best operational role (*P Richey via N Franks*)

Seen here planning an operation, Wg Cdr Denys Gillam led the first Typhoon Wing, and would later command No 146 Wing, famous for its devastating attacks on German HQs and other pinpoint targets. He finished the war with the DSO and two bars, DFC and bar and an AFC (*D E Gillam via N Franks*)

Sqn Ldr Paul Richey's personal Typhoon was R7752 'PR-G', which is seen here in the summer of 1942. Richey favoured 'G' throughout his combat career (he had flown Hurricane I 'JX-G' in France), and his Typhoon sported a red tip to the spinner, as had his earlier No 609 Sqn Spitfire. Note that the fuselage roundel has been modified to Type 'C' but the underwing roundel remains in the equally proportioned type 'A' style (*via G Seager*)

One of No 609 Sqn's early Typhoons, R7855 'PR-D' is seen around August 1942 prior to the application of any special markings. Note the individual letter 'D' repeated on the inner leading edge possibly in red (the flight colour), with a black outline. This aircraft would become the favoured mount of 'Cheval' Lallemant (*R P Beamont*)

designed and fitted, improvements made to the exhaust system and Napier sought the answer to the Sabre engine's frequent failures, two more squadrons were equipped with Typhoons, joining No 56 Sqn to become the Duxford Wing. In January 1942 No 266 'Rhodesian' Sqn exchanged its Spitfire VBs for Typhoon IAs, and in April, No 609 'West Riding' Sqn gave up its Spitfire VBs for the promising, but troublesome, fighter.

Commanding the unit at this time was Sqn Ldr Paul Richey, who was also a Battle of France ace with ten destroyed and one shared to his credit (also see *Osprey Aircraft of the Aces 18 - Hurricane Aces 1939-40* for further details). The Duxford Wing Leader was Denys Gillam, also an ace with seven and one shared destroyed, mostly with No 616 Sqn during the Battle of Britain (see *Osprey Aircraft of the Aces 12 - Spitfire Mk I/II Aces 1939-41* for further details). He had since commanded Nos 312 and 615 Sqns, both on Hurricanes. With the DSO and two DFCs already to his name, Gillam was a determined and capable leader.

Despite the best efforts of these seasoned pilots, the Typhoon's difficulties continued, with increasing numbers of engine failures and the first indications of structural problems. Meanwhile, the Wing worked steadily towards operational status, the first operational flight falling to No 266 Sqn on 28 May 1942 when a Typhoon was scrambled to investigate a 'Bogey' (which turned out to be a Spitfire).

Two days later, however, eight Typhoons of No 56 Sqn were detached (four to Manston and four to Tangmere) in the hope of intercepting Messerschmitt Bf 109s and Focke-Wulf Fw 190s of JGs 2 and 26 respectively (see *Osprey Aircraft of the Aces 9 - Fw 190 Aces of the Western Front* for further details). These two Luftwaffe *geschwader* were responsible for the 'hit and run' raids on the South Coast that had proved too fast for Fighter Command's Spitfires to intercept. The experiment soon proved to be a disaster, however, for when two Typhoons were scrambled to investigate an intruder, they were met by two Canadian Spitfires pursuing the same target. Mistaking the new aircraft for Fw 190s, the Spitfires opened fire and both unsuspecting Typhoons were shot down in the Channel. Only one of the pilots survived, albeit with burns.

The Typhoons returned to Snailwell (where No 56 Sqn had been based since March) and began to operate with the rest of the Duxford Wing. The first, uneventful, sweep was carried out on 20 June in support of 'Circus 193', but on 30 July disaster struck again when No 56 Sqn escorted Bostons to Abbeville. Returning early with engine trou-

Pilots of No 266 Sqn's 'A' Flight' pose for an informal group photo at Duxford in the summer of 1942. Second from the right, back row, is Plt Off N J Lucas, who shared the first Typhoon victory with Plt Off Munro (see below). At extreme right on the back row is Plt Off W Smithyman and, seated centre front, Flt Lt R Dawson, both of whom failed to return from a sweep in support of Operation *Jubilee* – the Dieppe landings of 19 August 1942 (*P W Penfold via A S Thomas*)

ble, Flg Off Erik Haabjoern, a Norwegian, was pounced on by Spitfires whose pilots had again mistaken his Typhoon for a Fw 190 – another Typhoon pilot ended up in the Channel.

Fortunately Erik survived, and although not destined to be an ace in air combat terms (although he would claim a Fw 190 and a Bf 109 destroyed, and a share in a Fw 200), he would become known as a fearless and aggressive Typhoon Wing leader. In fact, he would survive two more immersions in the Channel while leading No 124 Wing through the invasion period and the Normandy campaign.

DIEPPE

On 19 August 1942, the Typhoon's first big chance to prove itself in action arrived with the staging of Operation *Jubilee* – the infamous Dieppe landing – although the Duxford Typhoons were kept on the margins of the main action. The Wing operated at full three-squadron strength, undertaking three sweeps during the day, but only the second brought action. While Nos 56 and 609 Sqns had inconclusive encounters with Fw 190s, three No 266 Sqn pilots dived on Do 217s of KG 2. Rhodesian Flt Lt Dawson claimed one bomber destroyed, whilst a second was credited as a probable to Plt Off Munro (who had shared the first Typhoon victory). However, one of the Typhoons was not seen again, and on the return journey Spitfires, yet again, attacked the Hawker fighters. The victorious Flt Lt Dawson, hit by the first burst, plunged into the Channel and was lost.

This latter incident spawned a series of special marking for Typhoons. First came yellow wing bands, followed towards the end of 1942 by a white nose and black under-wing stripes. These in turn were soon replaced by the under-wing black and white stripes which proved effective, and characterised the Typhoon, throughout 1943.

Opinions on how the Typhoon could be best used were beginning to

After sharing in the first Typhoon victory, Plt Off Ian Munro was credited with a Do 217 probably destroyed at Dieppe. He subsequently perished in one of the numerous accidents attributed to structural failure when Typhoon EJ932 'ZH-N' disintegrated in a 520 mph dive and crashed near Exeter on 3 May 1943 (*P W Penfold via A S Thomas*)

polarise. The Engineering branch would have been happy to see the air-craft withdrawn altogether, as the effort required to keep the Sabre engines serviceable was enormous and, at that stage, out of all proportion to the successes achieved. Furthermore, structural failure of the rear fuselage, involving complete loss of the tail unit, was an increasing phenomenon.

Test pilots at the manufacturers and RAE Farnborough flew scores of terrifying sorties in an effort to replicate the conditions of the failure – there would have been little chance for the pilot had the failure actually occurred. Although elevator flutter was eventually isolated as the main cause, and modifications made to the elevator balances, it wasn't until the end of 1943 before the accident rate finally slowed, and even then some structural failures did occur. When Flt Lt J F L Sinclair on No 181 Sqn was killed on 18 July 1945, he was the last of 24 pilots to die in 26 known failures.

Few of the pilots, however, wished to see the Typhoon's service career ended. Gillam supported the continuation of traditional Wing tactics, Dundas thought there was still a role for the aircraft in large scale operations, while Richey wanted to exploit the potential of the Typhoon in special low-level operations. The Rhodesians of No 266 Sqn even threatened to resign their commissions if the Typhoon was withdrawn. Richey's view was supported by Fighter Command's Grp Capt Opera-tions, Harry Broadhurst, and inevitably the Duxford Wing was dispersed and the squadrons despatched to take up key positions along the east and a south coasts.

Meanwhile, new Typhoon squadrons were forming, Nos 257 and 486 Sqns trading in the their Hurricanes, while two completely new units, Nos 181 and 182 Sqns, took delivery of Typhoons config-ured for fighter-bomber operations. The way ahead for the aircraft was now apparent.

Wg Cdr Denys Gillam's Typhoon IB R7698 'Z-Z' at Duxford in the autumn of 1942. It shows signs of having been completely repainted in a non-standard pattern, which has also obscured the serial number. It features the small blister on the canopy roof (introduced about this time) housing a rear view mirror. The latter device subsequently proved to be of little use owing to the Typhoon's characteristic vibration (*D E Gillam*)

Filmed at Westhampnett (now Goodwood) in June 1942, Sqn Ldr 'Cocky' Dundas is seen taking off in Typhoon IA R7648 'US-A', which sports his pennant and the name *FARQUHAR IV* on the nose. The first 'anti-Rhubarb' patrols were flown from this South Coast base but proved fruitless (*IWM FLM 1480*)

JABO HUNTERS

In late September 1942, in the wake of Fighter Command's decision to use the Typhoon on low-level operations, the squadrons were re-deployed as single units at intervals along the coast. While the newly-equipped No 1 Sqn and No 56 Sqn remained at Acklington and Matlaske to cover the east coast, No 609 Sqn proceeded to the 'fighter Mecca', Biggin Hill, which served as the focal point of south-east air defences. Meanwhile, No 486 Sqn abandoned its Turbinlite trials and flew to North Weald, No 266 Sqn was positioned at Warmwell, in Dorset, and No 257 Sqn went to Exeter. The routine of flying 'anti-Rhubarbs' began, with pairs of Typhoons undertaking low-level patrols just off the coast that saw them positioned to counter the previously invulnerable *Jabos*.

Although success was not immediate, No 486 Sqn caught a Fw 190 of 10./JG 26 on 17 October and No 257 Sqn downed two more on 3 November. In December Nos 486 and 609 Sqns both moved nearer to the coast, to Tangmere and Manston respectively, and then the scoreboard began to fill. Fourteen claims (including three probables) were shared equally between Nos 486 and 609 Sqns – eight Fw 190s, four Bf 109s and two recce Do 217s.

Two of these claims, on 17 and 24 December 1942, were the first for Flt Sgt Frank Murphy, who would go on to become one of No 486 Sqn's most successful pilots, and narrowly miss becoming the first Typhoon ace. The first of these kills also involved Sgt K G 'Hyphen' Taylor-Cannon, who would also have a notable career with the New Zealand squadron.

On 17 December these two pilots were patrolling from Selsey to St Catherine's Point when they were

Pilots of No 486 Sqn RNZAF who destroyed seven enemy aircraft in the last weeks of 1942. The middle four, from left to right, are Flt Sgt Frank Murphy, Sgt 'Hyphen' Taylor-Cannon, Sgt 'Arty' Sames and Flg Off 'Spike' Umbers, and they would all make further claims. Both Taylor-Cannon and Umbers also later commanded the squadron (*via P Sortehaug*)

Sqn Ldr R P Beamont in the cockpit of R7752 'PR-G' in February 1943. Most of No 609 Sqn's Typhoons at this time carried the unit's white rose and hunting horns painted by the artist Eric Kennington (more famous for his pilot portraits). 'Bee's' scoreboard (only partially visible) shows five enemy aircraft and twenty locomotives destroyed (*IWM CH 18108*)

13

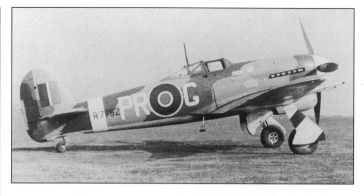

Beamont's Typhoon R7752 'PR-G', seen in March 1943 when the number of locos on the scoreboard had reached 23 – at the end of his tour the total was 25, and a ship had also been added. Since inheriting the aircraft from Paul Richey, the markings have changed – the serial number has been replaced, spinner and chin stripe painted yellow, cannon fairings added (also yellow), underwing roundels changed to type 'C' and underwing identity stripes added (*R P Beamont*)

vectored by 'Blackgang' (the low-looking radar on the Isle of Wight) onto two targets approaching St Catherine's Point on a north-easterly heading. Sighting two Bf 109s (now known to have been Bf 109F-4s from recce unit 4(F)./123) at zero feet, the Typhoon pilots gave chase as recorded in their combat report;

'At first the aircraft did not appear to see Red section which turned to port on to 060° and gave chase, they then turned South East and closing to about 300 yards clearly recognised them as ME109F's and opened fire with several shorter bursts of cannon closing still further, very rapidly (A.S.I. 350) to 100 yards in line abreast. (Enemy aircraft speed estimated 330). By this time all aircraft were right down "on the deck" and with the enemy aircraft adopting a spiral weave type of evasive action crossing over several times, as Red section attacked with the result that both Red 1 and 2 engaged each aircraft, strikes being observed on the fuselage and engine of both enemy aircraft. They soon abandoned the spiral weave action,

Pilots of No 609 Sqn at their Manston dispersal hut in the spring of 1943. Sqn Ldr Beamont stands in the centre of the doorway, whilst Flg Off Van Lierde is front row fourth from the left and Flg Off 'Cheval' Lallemant front row extreme right. Above the latter pilot is his No 2 in the epic combat of 14 February 1943, Flg Off Tony Polek. Above and left of Polek is Flt Sgt 'Pinkie' Stark, who later became an ace, and was also the last wartime CO of the 'West Riding' squadron (*via C Goss*)

No 486 Sqn's most successful pilot in the first six months of operations was Flt Sgt Frank Murphy (who rose to squadron leader rank). He destroyed three Bf 109s and a Ju 88, and thus narrowly missed becoming the first Typhoon ace with his claim for a Fw 190 probably destroyed on 15 July 1943 (*IWM CH 11580*)

No 266 Sqn pilots pose for a group shot at Exeter in July 1943. The CO, Sqn Ldr Charles Green, is standing in the centre (below the exhaust stacks of the Typhoon). By the time this photograph was taken his tour of operations was almost over, and he would, after a spell as Wing Commander (Tactics) at No 59 OTU, return to Typhoon operations as a Wing Leader
(*P W Penfold via A S Thomas*)

straightened out and flew parallel courses, apparently flat out.

'The plane subsequently destroyed by Red 2 (Taylor-Cannon) jettisoned its hood and with pieces breaking from it climbed to about 800 ft made a diving turn to starboard and went straight into the sea. The other, destroyed by a Red 1 (Murphy), with smoke pouring from its tanks, lowered its flaps, raised its nose slightly, burst into flames and dived into the water.'

The *Jabo* activity entered a new dimension when, on 20 January 1943, fighter-bombers (mainly from JG 26, but supplemented by others from JG 2 and the fighter school near Paris) executed a bold strike on London. The force, which was split into three waves, totalled 90 Bf 109s and Fw 190s. The first wave bombed London and largely escaped interception. The second wave, however, ran into stiffer opposition – especially the eight Bf 109Gs of 6./JG 26 which lost four of their number to a pair of No 609 Sqn Typhoons. One of the claiming pilots was Flg Off Johnny Baldwin, who was credited with three of the raiders (see Chapter Seven) in an unexpectedly high combat (for a Typhoon) at 20,000 ft. These were the first confirmed claims for Baldwin in a career which would see him end the war as the ranking Typhoon ace.

The *Jabo* campaign continued through February, with most claims going to No 609 Sqn. Another potential ace, Flg Off 'Cheval' Lallemant (one of No 609's Belgians), opened his account on the 14th during a patrol to protect a crippled MTB in the Channel. Four Fw 190s tore in to attack the boats, and Lallemant later described the hectic combat which resulted in his atmospheric biography, *Rendezvous with Fate*;

'Calling "Tally ho!" I lead Tony Polek into the attack, veering right to get into a firing position. Concentrating on their own attack, the 190s are unaware of our presence, and our Typhoons rapidly close the distance that separates us. I switch on my reflector-sight, control its adjustment, then grab the selector-switch of my camera gun. There is no answering noise when I press the button; the camera doesn't work – too bad!

'As we draw nearer we each have a target in front of us, and I measure the range in the reflector-sight. Just as it closes to six hundred yards, the sea around the enemy planes is spattered with explosions. It is Tony firing too soon and ruining the surprise. My fault; I have forgotten it is his first combat, and like every excited tenderfoot he has made the old mistake. I should have warned him. At once the 190s break in opposite directions, and instead of disposing of the hind pair and then engaging in equal combat with the other, we are now in a dangerous mess.

'The ensuing combat – two versus four – indeed waxes hotly. Fortunately there is cloud, and it may save us. The thing to do is to act quickly, taking advantage of the enemy's momentary disorganisation. So up we go in a climbing turn in pursuit of No 4. But this German seems a master pilot, and strive though I may, I just can't get his aircraft's image in my gun-sight. Up through the clouds, one behind the other, and when we emerge I am dazzled by the sun. The Focke-Wulf hesitates, then continues its upward soaring, and despite full boost I am lagging dangerously. If he gains much more distance I shall have to break off before it is too late – perhaps it is already. But suddenly the plane turns on its back and dives towards the clouds several thousand feet lower, and I gasp a sigh of relief.'

Photographed in front of his usual aircraft, EK243 'ZH-Q' (between May and September 1943), and burdened with parachute, helmet and mask, Flt Lt John Deall was No 266 Sqn's second Typhoon ace, achieving this status just one day after Norman Lucas. He would command the unit on his second tour, and finish the war as Wing Commander Flying, No 146 Wing. Note the pull down step to aid access to the cockpit and an open hand hold top right (*P W Penfold via A S Thomas*)

This picture certainly tells a story, summing up the Typhoon's problems at the end of 1942. The date is 25 November and the Typhoon is R8966 'XM-W' of No 182 Sqn, a victim of engine failure. It also displays the short-lived recognition markings – white nose and spinner and yellow wing bands. The pilot, Plt Off R Payne, has pulled of a successful forced landing at Bergholt, in Suffolk, and despite damage to the underside and starboard wingtip, R8966 would be repaired and returned to service (*No 182 Sqn records*)

Flt Sgt 'Babe' Haddon (left) and Sgt John Wiseman (with the dog) were two of No 609 Sqn's casualties in the battles over the Channel – both shot down while patrolling over a crippled MTB on 14 February 1943, although they were immediately avenged by Lallemant and Polek (see text). Typhoon R7713 'PR-Z' was part of No 609 Sqn's initial equipment, and survived more than a year of operations. The aircraft shows much sign of wear and tear and repainting. The black identity stripes have been extended over the cannon fairings (not normal practice), and the nose has non-standard camouflage as a result of painting out the unpopular white nose marking of November/December 1942, with a white strip remaining under the radiator fairing. The unit badge is just visible below the windscreen, and the rear half of the spinner, and 'Z' on the leading edge, both appear to be in the flight colour – presumably blue (*R A Lallemant via R Decobeck*)

This shot of a No 609 Sqn Typhoon in March 1943 makes an interesting comparison with the previous view of R7713. This aircraft (identity unknown), has factory-applied identity stripes, fully faired cannon barrels and a rear view mirror canopy blister, all of which suggest it is from the EJ/EK serial range which was delivered from February 1943 onwards. The light patch between the spinner and the radiator fairing indicates the aperture for the camera-gun, repositioned from the wing in a (not very successful) attempt to reduce vibration problems. Factory-finished Typhoons sported three grey cannons and one green (starboard outer) to match the upper surface camouflage pattern. The groundcrew are watching Sqn Ldr Beamont's 'PR-G' (note the yellow cannon barrels) flying overhead (*IWM CH 9252*)

Back through the clouds, Lallemant loses contact with everyone until;

'At last I see three aircraft break cloud: a Typhoon sandwiched between two Focke-Wulf 190s, the second firing at Tony, and Tony firing at the first. As they bank to starboard in Indian file just ahead of me, Tony's death is a few seconds away, but with all my speed it is all I can do to avoid collision. Clenched at the controls I struggle to join battle, trying to dictate my movements with my brain. But my muscles don't respond: instinct controls the emergency. My Typhoon is like a bolting horse, with me crouched on its withers. My thumb is on the firing button as I hurtle at right angles towards the mixed procession, and the black crosses of the enemy planes loom before me like a bank into which I am about to crash. And when I fire it is – contrary to all nature – with Tony in my gunsight.

'I see tracer shells. The deflection is terrific, and I would have given more but for fear of hitting Tony. The 190 is still firing at him, and better, I think, that he should be destroyed by the enemy than by me. But I am still firing too: just for two seconds before jerking the stick to avoid collision. But is it enough? As I break away the wing of the 190 explodes, and as it falls seawards Polek is at last safe. Banking to port, I see it swallowed up, leaving no trace but a swirl of water.'

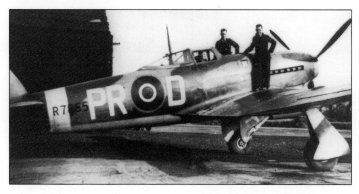

Flg Off 'Cheval' Lallemant is seen seated in the cockpit of his regular aircraft, R7855 'PR-D' of No 609 Sqn, at Manston in early 1943 (*R A Lallemant*)

Photographed at Matlaske on 21 April 1943, when the Typhoon was shown to the press for the first time, R8224 'US-H' of No 56 Sqn was one of the small batch (15) built by the parent company – most Typhoons (3300) were built by Gloster Aircraft. It was also a 'presentation' aircraft, carrying the name chosen by the donating organisation, *Land Girl*, beneath the cockpit. This view also displays the yellow wing bands to good advantage, and No 56 Sqn's style of extending them over the cannon fairing. Although not visible in this photo, R8224's identity stripes were incorrect, for the outer black and white stripes were missing from beneath each wing (*Aeroplane*)

The patrol resumed, and while making a final turn off Boulogne, a warning crackled on the R/T. 'Bandits approaching you from the east'. The Typhoons turn into the new threat – four yellow-nosed Fw 190s – and more are scrambled from Manston. With help on the way, Lallemant continued his second turning competition of the sortie;

'I sense that the German No 3 is feeling uncomfortable. In another half-turn, thanks to the manoeuvrability of my Typhoon, I shall have the chance to throw some lead at him. But he knows that too, and a second later quits the formation at a tangent – very annoying, for I can do nothing about it. Or can I? Tilting my aircraft, I touch the firing button for a split-second with a quite ludicrous amount of deflection, and at once resume my place in the turning circle, where my manoeuvre has already put me behind. The 190 is now hidden by the right wing of my banking Typhoon, but with luck I may have frightened it away. And then, just behind the trailing edge, there comes into view a flaming torch which a second later is doused forever in the sea.'

The locations of the Typhoon force had seen some changes in the last months of 1942 and the first of 1943. No 486 Sqn had been at Tangmere since October 1942 and No 609 Sqn at Manston since November, whilst Nos 257 and 266 Sqns had exchanged bases and No 1 Sqn had established itself at Lympne. There were changes on the other side of the Channel too. A new foe joined the battle in the spring of 1943 – *Schnellkampfgeschwader* 10. Formed in western France for employment against shipping in the Bay of Biscay, I. and II. *Gruppen* of SKG 10 had moved to Amiens to take over the *Jabo* role from JG 2 and JG 26, who were becoming more involved in defensive operations.

Although frequently encountered over the south-east, the *Jabos* did not confine their attention just to this corner of England. For example, on 10 January 1943 Flg Off Small of No 266 Sqn caught a Fw 190 of 10(*Jabo*)./JG 2 off Teignmouth, and on the 26th of the month Flg Off Bell despatched another from the same unit off Start Point. Exactly one month later No 266's CO, Sqn Ldr Charles Green, intercepted two more and sent them to watery graves 50 miles south of Exemouth. Green would not figure on any list of aces, but went on to become one of the great fighter-bomber leaders, firstly at the helm of No 121 Wing in Normandy, and then commanding No 124 Wing.

Another Rhodesian who would achieve ace status and high rank was Johnny Deall, who also made his mark at this time by despatching

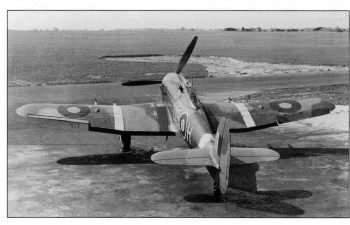

two Fw 190s from 5./SKG 10 on 13 March, the second being shared with Flt Sgt Eadie.

On 1 June 1943 Flg Off I J Davies of No 609 Sqn repeated Johnny Baldwin's feat of the previous January. While patrolling the coast as No 2 to Flt Lt Wells, he spotted bomb bursts in Margate, followed quickly by the culprits – four Fw 190s in line astern. SKG 10 in action again. Davies' combat report detailed the subsequent events;

'I dived down to these firing a short burst 4-500 yds and managed to get in a 2 sec. burst from 2-300 yds at the last one as he was gunning the gas holder and Broadstairs streets. Seeing a formation of 6 FW 190s heading out to sea at 0 feet I gave chase to these. As I crossed the coast I passed the FW 190 already attacked and saw it jettison a black object, probably its hood, followed by what appeared to be the legs of the pilot trying to get out. The six Huns I was after were in a vic of five with one in the box. Selecting this one I fired a burst from 500-600 yds and he obligingly weaved which enabled me to close and give him further bursts which spattered the sea until I was at 200 yds range, finishing with a 2-3 second burst dead on.

'Just then I was conscious of red and yellow tracer passing much too close over my wings from behind so I turned sharply to port just as the Hun I had fired at crashed into the sea with a great fountain of water. I did a 360 degs turn and finding nothing in sight continued on my previous course all out, and soon saw two FW 190s with another to port. I chose this one which climbed to 200 ft as we approached Ostende, and closing to 150-200 yds fired a 1 sec burst which finished my ammo. I saw strikes

Photographed on the same occasion as the previous aircraft, R8220 'US-D' (another Hawker-built machine) is seen with its engine cowls removed and fitters working on the Sabre engine. Half obscured by the fitter's leg is a badge showing a diving Typhoon, marked 'US-D', shattering a swastika and captioned 'Shape of things to come'. Note the yellow leading edge stripe terminates just after the outer cannon (*Aeroplane*)

Another shot taken on the Typhoon's press day sees a formation of No 56 Sqn aircraft airborne for the photographers' benefit. Nearest is EK183 'US-A', whilst others in the formation also include R8825 'US-Y', DN317 'US-C', R8224 'US-H', R8721 'US-X' and R8220 'US-D' (*Aeroplane*)

on the cockpit and port wing, from which a large piece dropped off, and then the Hun burst into flames and black smoke poured out.

'The other two 190s had by now turned to attack, so I turned sharply home, and crossing in at Deal, landed at base.'

Meanwhile, Wells had joined a formation of 12 Fw 190s racing for home. He despatched two before the others realised, and turned in to attack him. Ammunition exhausted, he climbed steeply out of danger and turned for home. This would be the last time the Luftwaffe fighter-bombers would be seen over the UK in any strength, but although SKG 10 had been badly mauled, they were not defeated. However, their ranks were greatly reduced in number, with Stab., II. and IV./SKG 10 being posted to Sicily, leaving just 1./SKG 10 with 30 Fw 190s on the Channel front. In fact the Typhoons would not meet SKG 10 in the defensive role again, although they would clash as the former took up the offensive.

The last Fw 190s destroyed by Typhoon coastal defenders were from reconnaissance unit NAGr 13, and they fell to No 266 Sqn. Two aircraft were intercepted on 15 October 1943, and both were shot down into the sea 40 miles off Start point. One of the claiming pilots was Flg Off N J Lucas (one and a share), who had shared in the first successful Typhoon air combat some 14 months earlier.

Although the huge effort of maintaining the patrols had been well rewarded, the period was also one of frustration for many Typhoon pilots, who carried out countless unrewarded sorties. Between mid October 1942 and 1 June 1943 no less than 42 Fw 190s and 15 Bf 109s were claimed destroyed, whilst eight more Fw 190s and two Bf 109s were claimed as probables. No 609 Sqn accounted for 27 confirmed kills out of the above total, followed by Nos 486 and 266 Sqns with 14 and 6 respectively. Tying for the title of top scoring pilot was Frank Murphy of No 486 Sqn and No 609 Sqn pilots 'Cheval' Lallemant and Johnny Baldwin. Who would be the first Typhoon ace?

By the autumn of 1943, standing patrols had been reduced and replaced by pairs of Typhoons at readiness. These two are JP447 'FM-C' and JP494 'FM-D' at Warmwell. Both aircraft have their individual letters ('C' and 'D') repeated on the leading edge and radiator fairing respectively (*IWM CH 11993*)

Harrowbeer, 15 October 1943, and Flg Off Norman Lucas (facing the camera, partly obscured by another pilot), fresh from downing a Fw 190 of NAGr 13, and sharing in the destruction of a second, gives fellow pilots the 'gen'. His Typhoon is JP906 'ZH-L', which was one of the late JP/early JR-serialled aircraft fitted with whip aerials and exhaust fairings (*via M Schoeman*)

'RHUBARBS' AND 'RANGERS'

Whilst the resource-consuming anti-'Rhubarb' work had been the Typhoon's prime role since the end of 1942 to mid-1943, proponents of the aircraft had not been content to leave other roles unexplored. Foremost among these was Roland 'Bee' Beamont, veteran of both the Battles' of France and Britain. With four destroyed, one shared destroyed and a probable to his credit, he had spent a rest tour with Hawker Aircraft as a test pilot, helping develop the Typhoon. Convinced of the aircraft's potential, 'Bee' had joined No 56 Sqn in mid-1942 as a supernumerary flight lieutenant, but soon took over a flight on No 609 Sqn, before taking command when Paul Richey went on rest.

Beamont had experience of night intruder work with No 87 Sqn on Hurricanes, and conducted trials to see if the Typhoon could be used in the same way. After taking command of No 609 Sqn, he undertook a moonlight 'Rhubarb' that saw him find and attack a train near Abbeville – the first of many 'brewed up' by the unit. In fact, by the time Beamont's partnership with R7752 'PR-G' (his regular mount during this period) was finally over, 25 small locomotive symbols were displayed beneath the cockpit. The original panel can still be seen today in the RAF Museum.

Under Beamont's direction, No 609 Sqn undertook training to enable regular and effective intruder sorties to be flown by day or by night, and in a burgeoning programme, had attacked some 25 trains by the end of December 1942. These operations continued into 1943, and on one of them Beamont was presented with his best chance to add to his air combat record whilst flying Typhoons. Taking off from Manston at 2000 hours on 18 January to patrol Creil airfield, he was attracted by a searchlight cone and anti-aircraft fire north of Dover. His combat report by the squadron Intelligence Officer continues;

'He saw a T.E. (twin-engined) aircraft 1000 feet above and to starboard, and identified it as a Ju.88 heading S. A.A. fire ceased and assisted by the S/Ls (searchlights), one of which illuminated e/a (enemy aircraft) by reflection, he attacked from slightly below and 30 degs. Firing a 3-4 sec. burst from 400 closing to 200 yds. Strikes were

Sqn Ldr Desmond Scott, CO of No 486 Sqn, is seen sitting in the cockpit of his Typhoon, EJ981 'SA-F', at Tangmere in July 1943. He shot down a Fw 190, and shared in the destruction of another, while flying this aircraft (*IWM CH 10620*)

Battle of France and Britain ace, and subsequently an evader, Denis Crowley-Milling took command of the first Typhoon fighter-bomber unit, No 181 Sqn, when it formed in September 1942. In June 1943 he took his squadron to Tangmere to introduce the Typhoon fighter-bomber to the press, which is when this photo was taken. He is seen climbing into the cockpit of his own aircraft, EK270 'EL-X', which sports the unofficial unit badge also carried by other Typhoons in the unit. A pair of 500-lb bombs, as seen here, remained the maximum load for the Typhoon until the summer of 1944, when the aircraft was cleared for the carriage of two 1000-lb bombs (*Aeroplane*)

seen on the fuselage and port wing, and a puff of smoke. E/a made a violent climbing turn into cloud 200 ft. above.'

Despite the fact that the plot faded from screens at the same time, Beamont was only able to claim a 'damaged'.

On the same day that 'Bee' had made his first night attack, No 56 Sqn had flown their first day 'Rhubarb', crossing the North Sea to attack an airfield near Vlissingen (Plt Off Deugo had flown so low during the sweep that he had killed a German gunner with the leading edge of his Typhoon's wing). With practical demonstrations of the Typhoon's potential such as these, confidence in the aircraft grew, and eventually the critics were silenced.

Heavy commitment to the endless anti-'Rhubarb' patrols limited the availability of Typhoons to undertake offensive operations in the first half of 1943, but during this period several more squadrons joined the two already mentioned – Nos 181 and 182 – in the fighter-bomber role. Usually these squadrons were escorted by fighter Typhoons, but even so, intent on their targets, they often suffered losses. The hunter had become the hunted. Shipping, from the Dutch coast to Brittany, became a regular target, but these dangerous sorties (vessels were usually protected by deadly flak ships) brought few opportunities for air combat.

One of the units regularly employed as escort on these occasions was No 486 Sqn, led since April 1943 by Sqn Ldr Desmond Scott. The latter was an experienced Hurricane pilot with three and one shared, four probables and four damaged already to his credit, and his aggressive leadership would bring him further successes while flying Typhoons. As early as 9 April he claimed shares in a probable and a damaged Fw 190 – the pair had attempted to attack his formation of four Typhoons near Etretat.

Five days later he shared in the destruction of a Bf 109, and on 25 May destroyed a Fw 190 some 30 miles south of Brighton. The latter was one of twelve aircraft returning from an SKG 10 attack on the city. The formation was 'flat out on the deck' but Scott, scrambled from Tangmere, was able to overhaul one of two stragglers and employ the usual technique. As the target came within maximum range, a burst of cannon fire gave the enemy pilot a stark choice – remain a sitting duck or weave – but weaving caused the range to close more quickly. This pilot chose the latter option, and soon his Fw 190 was cart-wheeling into the Channel.

On 24 June Scott had a novel experience – two combats against Fw 190s, the first one RAF flown, the second Luftwaffe! The former was probably PE882 (a SKG 10 aircraft which had landed at West Malling in

error some two months previously) from RAE Farnborough. Scott had this to say about the encounter;

'I engaged in a mock combat with the 190 in the skies above Sussex and was surprised by its speed and manoeuvrability. But I was confident I could get the better of it, providing we remained below 10,000 ft. Above that altitude it was a different story. The higher we went the more like a carthorse I became. However, since we were essentially on low-attack ops, our chances of becoming embarrassed at 10,000 ft or above were remote.'

His chance to put his findings to the test came in the afternoon. Returning from escorting Typhoon fighter-bombers to Abbeville, and pursued by Fw 190s which were unable to close, the formation was suddenly attacked by two more which seemed to appear from nowhere;

'I quickly broke to starboard. The FW 190s foolishly dived under us towards the sea, and this gave us the immediate advantage. I took a quick look round while sprinting down after them. Fitz, my No 2, was hanging on to my tail, and I could see nothing else close to me except our own

On 6 July 1943, 16-kill Hurricane ace Wg Cdr A C Rabagliati, Wing Commander Flying Coltishall, borrowed Sqn Ldr Don 'Butch' Taylor's Typhoon to lead a shipping strike. Hit by flak off the Dutch coast, Rabagliati was forced to bale out 60 miles off Great Yarmouth, and despite a massive air and sea search, no trace of him was ever found. As the squadron OC's aircraft, EK273 was unusual in that it displayed his initials in lieu of an individual letter, as well as No 195 Sqn's allotted 'JE' codes (*K A J Trott*)

As four of No 609 Sqn's most successful pilots, this quartet were each awarded DFCs in the autumn of 1943. They are, from left to right, Flg Off Remy (also known as 'Mony' Van Lierde), Plt Off 'Pinkie' Stark, Flg Off Charles Demoulin ('Windmill Charlie') and Flt Lt Johnny Baldwin. The middle two would both later command No 609 Sqn, whilst the others eventually led units in the same Wing (*L W F Stark*)

23

Typhoons. Within seconds I was firing directly down on a FW 190. He turned to port close to the water. My deflection was astray – I could see cannon shells splashing in the sea just behind his tail. Suddenly we were at the same level and locked in a desperate battle to out-turn each other.

'I applied the pressure to get my sights ahead of him, but I kept losing my vision as the blood was forced away from my head; a little less pressure on the control column would bring my sight back into focus. I could see him looking back at me on the other side of our tight circle. I knew he was experiencing the same effects, and although I could feel my aircraft staggering, I continued to apply the pressure. I was beginning to gain on him, but I was still well off the required deflection. With my heart pounding in my throat, I applied some top rudder to get above him. Just as I did so, his wings gave a wobble and he flicked over and hit the sea upside-down.

'I saw the great shower of spray his aircraft sent up, but not much else. I blacked out, went out of control myself, and recovered from my downward plunge just clear of the water. According to Fitz I had spun upwards. It could easily have been the other way, and both my Luftwaffe opponent and I would have finished up under water.'

During the same action, 'Spike' Umbers was also credited with a Fw 190 destroyed. This was his first solo confirmed kill, having previously shared a Do 217, a probable and a damaged Fw 190. He would become one of the few aces with all claims on Typhoons and Tempests.

Sqn Ldr Scott's policy of taking the war to the enemy sometimes had unexpected consequences. While searching for elusive E-boats on 14 July, he spotted two dinghies carrying 11 American airmen, who were eventually rescued by an ASR launch. Setting out the next morning to resume the search for the E-boats, another bomber crew in their dinghy was sighted just off Le Havre. Leaving four Typhoons circling the downed airmen, Scott returned to Tangmere and organised an ASR Hudson to deliver a lifeboat to the bomber crew. The Hudson was escorted back to Le Havre and the drop accomplished successfully, but on the return journey the Luftwaffe finally put in an appearance;

'I looked up and sure enough the duck-egg blue bellies of a pack of Huns were circling directly above. They had the drop on us and I had the feeling normally associated with nakedness. But they did not seem keen

Flt Lt Erik Haabjoern, 'A' Flight commander of No 609 Sqn, is seen with DN360 'PR-A' after successfully belly-landing at Manston on 1 June 1943 following flak damage while attacking shipping near Vlissingen. Promoted soon after to command No 247 Sqn, he would later lead No 124 Wing during the D-Day invasion. DN360 was probably the most successful Typhoon ever built in terms of aerial success, being credited with five victories, including three by Johnny Baldwin on 20 January 1943 and a Fw 190 by Haabjoern on 9 April 1943 (*via C Goss*)

to take the plunge. The others had returned to Tangmere by this time, so we made eight in all.

'I slowly circled away from the lifeboat, and when we were well clear of it, I instructed the boys to follow me and listen carefully for my command to "break". As soon as I straightened out, and we were more or less back in our pairs, the 109s and 190s pounced down on us. At the first sign of tracer I yelled out "Break!" and swung up to port. I realised immediately that I had forgotten something when a 190 overshot and crossed to starboard right in front of me. I pressed the firing button, and as he flew through my fire I hit his slipstream and was thrown into a spin. Of all my close squeaks this must have been the closest, for in recovering I almost collected the pilot of the Fw 190 as he was thrown from his aircraft, a split second before the plane hit the sea. This spin-off was of my own making. While mentally mapping out my tactics I had forgotten to move my coarse cruising pitch into fine position. I never saw any of my cannon shells hit this aircraft, although Fitz (who shared the claim), in close attendance as usual, was sure they had. Jim McCaw, was also near to me, said later that my prop missed hitting the water by inches.'

In this combat Frank Murphy came close to being the first Typhoon ace, scoring strikes on a Fw 190 which fled towards France trailing thick smoke – he was credited with a probable only. 'Arty' Sames also claimed a Fw 190 destroyed, this being his third kill (the first one being shared), and although he would not add to his score, he would later become the only Typhoon V1 ace on a second tour with No 137 Sqn.

As mentioned earlier, Typhoon offensive ops had been pioneered by No 609 Sqn. This initiative, started by Beamont, was fostered by the next CO, Sqn Ldr Alec Ingle (another Battle of Britain veteran with two destroyed, three probables and a damaged to his credit while serving with No 605 Sqn), despite the restriction that was put on Typhoon flying hours. Officially rationed to 300 hours per month due to the shortage of serviceable engines, the unit bent the rules to keep their private war going.

One of their best exponents of the art was Remy Van Lierde (usually known as 'Mony'), a Belgian who had escaped the German occupation of his country by fleeing to England, where he had learnt to fly with the RAF. He had opened his score on 20 January 1943 when, in the aftermath of the big *Jabo* attack on London, he shot down a Fw 190 at 27,000 ft – surely the highest ever successful Typhoon combat. Literally at home when on 'Rhubarbs' over Belgium, his next success was on 26 March 1943 when he encountered a Ju 52 near Ath – it was swiftly despatched. Night 'Rhubarbs' were Van Lierde's speciality, and after bombing an enemy airfield on the night of 14/15 May, he spotted a He 111 in the gloom, causing it to crash as it attempted evasive action.

Sqn Ldr Mike Bryan of No 198 Sqn studies the damage to the wing of his Typhoon, JP666 'TP-N', caused by a 20 mm flak hit during a shipping strike off the Dutch coast on 27 September 1943. He was forced to touch down at 140 knots, as the Typhoon was uncontrollable below that speed (*IWM CH 12812*)

Sqn Ldr 'Ronnie' Fokes (centre) completed a very successful tour with No 92 Sqn during and following the Battle of Britain (nine and four shared destroyed, two unconfirmed destroyed, three probables and one and one shared damaged). Despite a spell as a flight commander with No 56 Sqn, and a full tour as CO of No 257 Sqn, he had no chance to add to his score. He was shot down by flak and baled out too low shortly after D-Day, already overdue a rest from operations (*No 257 Sqn records*)

Pilots of No 182 Sqn gather round to view the flak damage to Plt Off 'Sandy' Allen's Typhoon, EK195 'XM-B', at Appledram on 21 June 1943
(*J A Sandeman Allen via B H Cull*)

On 30 July 1943, six of No 609 Sqn's Typhoons escorted Bostons to bomb Schipol airfield. Just off the Dutch coast, the Typhoons were 'bounced' by Spitfires, who were in turn being 'jumped' by Bf 109s! In the combat that followed, Erik Haabjoern managed to shoot down one Bf 109 and Van Lierde was credited with the destruction of another, which crashed into the sea attempting to follow his highly evasive flying. This brought the Belgian's total to four confirmed.

In August 1943 Alec Ingle departed upon being promoted to Wing Commander Flying (WCF), No 124 Airfield, No 16 Wing. However, within a few weeks he would be a PoW, having been shot down by 4./JG 26's commanding officer, Leutnant Hoppe, while taking part in a three-squadron attack on Beauvaistille. Also involved in the operation were two other aces, namely Wg Cdr Denis Crowley-Milling (WCF No 121 Airfield) and Grp Capt H de C A 'Paddy' Woodhouse, (OC No 16 Wing). The latter pilot claimed a damaged (to add to his three and two shared destroyed and three damaged, mostly as Tangmere Wing Leader), along with similar claims by two other members of the formation.

At the same that Sqn Ldr Ingle departed No 609 Sqn, the unit also had Flt Lt Erik Haabjoern posted away to lead his own Typhoon unit. However, waiting in the wings to make good these losses were two quality replacements. Johnny Baldwin, with his proven track record on the unit, became the new 'A' Flight commander, whilst the new CO (yet another forward-looking leader) was Pat Thornton-Brown, who had previously flown Whirlwinds, before becoming a flight commander on No 56 Sqn.

He soon latched on to the possibilities opened up by the development of long-range tanks for the Typhoon. These carried 44 gallons apiece, and with one under each wing, the aircraft's range was extended by a very useful 400 miles (provided they were dropped when empty). Top speed was reduced by about 30 mph when the tanks were carried, but they could be jettisoned, of course, should action demand.

This facility would bring nightfighter and training bases (previously out of range for RAF fighters) within the sphere of operations for the Typhoon units. On 8 August Flt Lt L E Smith proved the potential of the tanks by becoming the first Typhoon pilot to penetrate German airspace with a record-breaking long-range 'Rhubarb' that saw him fly in through Holland and out via Belgium.

The tanks were not readily available, however, and Thornton-Brown had to fight to acquire two more pairs. When they finally materialised, a sortie to the west of Paris with Baldwin that resulted in two Fw 190s being destroyed, set the pattern for the coming months. The Focke-Wulf brought Baldwin's score to five destroyed, thus making him the first Typhoon ace. Over the coming months he would maintain his position as top-scorer.

In August 1943 No 609 Sqn were joined at Manston by another Typhoon squadron, No 198. It was commanded by ex-Whirlwind pilot Mike Bryan, who had shares in a Do 217 destroyed and a Fw 190 probable to his credit. September was a quiet month for air combat, but from October through to February 1944, the two units enjoyed a run of success, mainly on 'Rangers', which became the envy of Fighter Command.

On 4 October Baldwin added to his score with a Fw 190 destroyed, and the next day Van Lierde reached ace status with a Ju 88. Some three hours earlier in the day, Plt Off 'Pinkie' Stark also made a significant claim when he destroyed a Ju 88. This was added to his Fw 190 kill from the previous March. The combat reports give some idea of the hectic action on a 'Ranger'. Stark and Flg Off 'Arty' Ross had left Lympne at 1317 hrs;

'Proceedings S. From Soissons, they came to turn A/F. in a flat wooded area, about 70 miles E. of Paris. This is believed to have been Connantre. On it was about 8 ME.110s. Three of these were in a row, 1 being refuelled. P/O. Stark fired a burst at the middle one, seeing strikes, whereupon the port engine and cockpit burst into flames and the servicing party scattered. F /O. Ross attacked an ME.110 in a different part of the airfield. Though hampered by the fact that his reflector sight was u/s, he saw strikes all around his target and must have hit it. Flak having started, the pilots did not tarry, they continued straight on S. About one minute later a JU.88 was sighted at 3000 ft, 5 miles to Starboard, going N. Stark made a sharp climbing turn and when he was a 1/2 mile behind and 1000 ft below E/A turned east; when he had closed range to 400 yds, E/A

The survival odds for flight and squadron commanders of Typhoon units were not too good, as this group shot proves. In the centre of the photo is Sqn Ldr Pheloung of No 56 Sqn, who was shot down by flak on a shipping strike on 20 June 1943. To the right of the CO is Flt Lt Pat Thornton-Brown (two and three shared destroyed and two shared damaged), who later took command of No 609 Sqn and was shot down by USAAF P-47s on 21 December 1943. To the left of Pheloung is Flt Brian Hawkins, who had already been shot down over France and evaded while flying Hurricanes with No 245 Sqn by the time this shot was taken. He would, however, survive his tour with No 56 Sqn on Typhoons and return to fly Tempests in 1945 (*BAe*)

Plt Off 'Pinkie' Stark had reason to smile, having just claimed No 609 Sqn's 200th victory, and won the not inconsiderable sweepstake, which had been awaiting the lucky pilot, in the process . . .

turned slowly North again. The first burst set the starboard engine on fire and E/A began turning and going down. At 500 ft. it levelled out again, flying South. A second burst from 100 yds produced smoke from the other engine and strikes on the cockpit. Stark overshot, but saw E/A crash into a wood and catch fire, after the hood had been jettisoned and one occupant jumped out just above the ground.'

The victory was significant because it was No 609's 200th, and provided the excuse for a huge party in the Hotel Majestic in Folkestone, which was attended by over 600 guests!

Van Lierde had set off, with fellow Belgian Sgt Watelet, about an hour after Stark and Ross returned. Losing contact with his leader, Watelet abandoned the sortie, but Van Lierde pressed on, eventually finding an airfield about 60 miles south of Paris, where he attacked two Ju 88s on the ground. Proceeding to the Laon/Soissons area, he surprised another Ju 88 preparing to land. Opening fire, he saw hits on the tail and cockpit before the airfield flak opened up, also scoring hits on the luckless Ju 88! The German bomber pulled up and then crashed on its side, narrowly missing its tormentor in its final plunge.

On the last day of the following month, Van Lierde made his final claim. In his year with No 609 Sqn he had already been responsible for the destruction of five different types of enemy aircraft – Fw 190, Ju 52, He 111, Bf 109, Ju 88 and now a sixth, a Bf 110, appropriately over his beloved Belgium. His tour was completed in December, but he would soon see further action on Tempests, and then Typhoons again.

This was also the day that No 198 Sqn made its mark, Mike Bryan leading nine long-range Typhoons on a sweep across Holland. It was Bryan's last trip with the unit, and Red 2 was none other than Johnny Baldwin, who had been promoted and was about to take his place. Unfortunately Baldwin's Sabre engine began cutting out, forcing him to return with an escort – and thus miss the 'Ranger' pilot's dream.

Sweeping round to approach Deelen from the north due to bad weather to the south, the Typhoons quickly spotted a Ju 188, which was attacked by Yellow section, led by Flt Lt V Smith – his shooting fatally damaged the Junkers, but the rest of the section poured more cannon fire into the doomed aircraft. The formation resumed course for Deelen, and was greeted with the sight of three pairs of Fw 190s in the circuit preparing to land. As the leading Focke-Wulf touched down, Bryan tackled the German's No 2, which rolled over and crashed east of the runway threshold. Bryan's No 2 'hosed' the leading Fw 190 as it left the runway, leaving it stopped and smoking. Flt Lt Fittall and Flg Off Williams despatched the second pair of Focke-Wulfs, and one of the third pair fell to Flg Off Abbott. The entire battle took about four minutes. On to Gilze-Rijen, which offered no targets, but a barge, tug and dredger all received attention on the way home.

Nine Typhoons of No 198 Sqn

. . . the victim was a Ju 88 (as seen by his gun-camera) encountered at low level on a 'Ranger' south of Soissons on 5 October 1943 (both photos L W F Stark)

Promoted to lead the Tangmere Wing, Wg Cdr Des Scott is seen posing alongside his Typhoon, R8843, which carried his initials. This was the first Typhoon with the sliding hood, which did so much to improve visibility from the cockpit, to reach an operational unit. Supplies were slow at first, and such aircraft remained the privilege of squadron and flight commanders on most units well into 1944 (*D J Scott*)

set out again on 4 December on a 'Fortress Support Sweep' ('Ramrod 348'). They rendezvoused with No 609 Sqn over North Foreland, who were providing top cover to their Manston neighbours on this occasion.

At Eindhoven No 198 Sqn encountered four Do 217s in line abreast and waded in, claiming all four destroyed – one of these provided Baldwin with yet another victory. Meanwhile, at a lower altitude, No 609 Sqn had also found a number of KG 2's Dorniers, and Pat Thornton-Brown and 'Arty' Ross each claimed one apiece, and shared a third. The latter pilot also shared another Do 217 with Sgt Henrion, whilst two other Belgians, Flg Off Geerts and Plt Off Detal, claimed one and two destroyed respectively. Eleven in all! A KG 2 veteran remarked after the war, 'I thanked my stars I was not flying that day!'

Down in the south-west, No 266 Sqn, now based at Harrowbeer near Plymouth, were also taking advantage of the increase in range offered by the arrival of external tanks. They were now led by Peter Lefevre, who had seen action in Norway, the Battle of Britain and Malta, flying with Nos 46 and 126 Sqns – his score stood at four and three shared destroyed, one shared probable and one damaged.

On 1 December he led an escort of Typhoons from his own unit, and No 193 Sqn, to cover a shipping strike off the southern Brittany coast. The first enemy aircraft encountered during the operation was a lumbering 'mausi' Ju 52 from one of the *Minensuchgruppen* based on the west coast of France. It was quickly despatched. Two Ju 88s followed, Lefevre sharing one with three of his pilots, whilst the other was split between Nos 193 and 266 Sqns. One of the claimants for the latter was Johnny Deall, who had shot down one of the SKG 10 raiders, and shared in the destruction of another, the previous March. He would further add to this score before finishing his tour early in 1944. On a similar sortie at the end of the month Flg Off N J Lucas claimed his fourth kill, sharing another minesweeping Ju 52 with a No 266 Sqn pilot near the Isle de Groix.

The period was not without its setbacks, however. On 21 December No 609 Sqn lost their irrepressible leader Pat Thornton-Brown, and the manner of his going made the loss even worse. Detailed as close escort to USAAF Marauders, two Typhoons were allocated to each 'box' of the medium bombers. Once more the old recognition problem reared its head, and two of the Typhoons (including Thornton-Brown's) were shot down by USAAF Thunderbolts. The CO baled out successfully, only to be shot and killed while descending by German ground forces. His replacement was Johnny Wells, a No 609 Sqn 'old boy' whose score stood at three destroyed and one damaged when he assumed command.

The New Year began with Typhoon pilots from Nos 198 and 609 Sqns hogging the limelight again. On 2 January a No 198 Sqn 'Ranger' to the west of Paris found more ground targets – Bf 110s and Me 210s – on a Luftwaffe airfield, but on the return journey a number of Bu 131 trainers were surprised over Paris and chased around the Eiffel Tower! One was shot down and another damaged, whilst the rest proved too elusive. A Fw 190 that was also encountered was less fortunate, falling to Sqn Ldr Baldwin's guns. The following day Flg Off Charles Detal shot down a Fw 190, which was his fourth claim in three months. He would bag three more before the end of the month, making him the fastest scoring Typhoon ace.

On 4 January Nos 198 and 609 Sqns set out in force (with seven and nine Typhoons respectively) on a 'Ranger' in support of 'Ramrod 421'. The plan was to fly at 'zero feet' to Gilze-Rijen airfield (which, by a strange twist of fate, would be their base in less than a year), where they would separate. No 609 would then cover Volkel and Deelen airfields, whilst No 198 Sqn would 'visit' Eindhoven and Venlo.

Approaching Gilze-Rijen, the Typhoon pilots spotted a Do 217 and followed it to the airfield. There followed a scene reminiscent of that played out at Eindhoven a month earlier – No 609 Sqn were credited with four Do 217s (plus two more and an unidentified aircraft, believed to have been a Ju 88C, on the ground) to No 198 Sqn's single claim. 'Pinkie' Stark shared one of the Dorniers for his fourth victory.

The rest of the Typhoon force (by January 1944 there were some 19 squadrons so equipped) missed out on much of this action. Since the end of November 1943, many of these units had been engaged in a less glamorous campaign against the 'Noball' sites – constructions intended for the launching of V1 flying bombs. This commitment continued into the spring of 1944, although most 2nd TAF Typhoon Wings (which were now forming) would get the chance to try their hand at 'Rangers', albeit with less spectacular success. The Luftwaffe was becoming harder to find.

Meanwhile, Nos 198 and 609 Sqns continued chalking up their victories. Mike Bryan took time off from his staff job to fly with his old squadron on occasions, and both he and Baldwin shot down ex-*Armée de l'Air* Caudron-Goeland transports on 13 January. Eleven days later Flg Off Geoff Eagle of No 198 Sqn (who had at least two destroyed, a probable and three damaged from a tour flying Hurricane Mk IIs with No 274 Sqn in the Western Desert) joined the select band of Typhoon pilots who claimed three destroyed in a single sortie.

Eagle was part of a formation of no less than 24 Typhoons, drawn from Nos 3, 198 and 609 Sqns, that had detached to Coltishall for the day. They had been tasked with escorting Coastal Command Beaufighters on a shipping strike off the Frisian Islands, but when the 'Beaus' arrived over Coltishall two minutes early and then failed to orbit, only elements of No

Flg Off Geoff Eagle single-handedly attacked a dozen Bf 109s, claiming three, on 24 January 1943. Having seen service in North Africa flying Hurricanes with No 274 Sqn and making several claims, this brought his score to at least five (possibly seven) destroyed, one probable and two or three damaged. He was killed shortly after the war while conducting propeller trials for de Havilland when his Typhoon suffered structural failure and crashed near Brockenhurst (*via N Franks*)

3 Sqn and four aircraft from No 198 Sqn managed to make contact. The rest were forced to return after 20 minutes fruitless searching.

Part of the latter group, Eagle had chosen to continue on course on his own in the hope of catching the main formation. In this he was unsuccessful, but about 30 miles north of Ameland, flying at zero feet, he ran into 12 Bf 109Gs! They were flying in three sections of four, in a shallow vic, at 300 ft, approaching from port on a course at right angles to his own. His combat report read as follows;

'I broke port and attacked the Squadron leader with a short burst from 300 yards and at 90 degs allowing some $3^1/2$ rings deflection for target speed of 260-280 m.p.h. This produced cannon strikes on his belly jettison tank, and caused it to explode and envelop the entire aircraft with blazing fuel, sending it plunging into the sea.

'Maintaining same line of flight and deflection I transferred my aim to No. 3 of same section, firing a longer burst while closing from 200-80 yards. For a while I saw nothing, then a strike caused an issue of grayish-white smoke from the cockpit. Hun immediately lurched to port, collided with his No. 4 and took both of them down to join their late leader.'

One of the other two sections made a half-hearted attempt at a head-on attack as Eagle broke to port, before joining the other section in running for home with 'black throttle smoke' streaming from their exhausts! This left the sole survivor of the first section who, after an unsuccessful attempt to turn on to Eagle's tail, also ran for home, leaving the Typhoon pilot to set course for Coltishall. These three kills brought Eagle a DFC, as well as ace status. He completed his operational tour, only to perish a few days after the end of the war in the penultimate Typhoon crash through structural failure.

Three days later two more Typhoon aces were created when 'Pinkie' Stark and Charles Detal undertook a 'Rhubarb' to Brussels. First victim for Detal was a 'silver' Bf 110 of Erla Brussels (a repair organisation), then more similar aircraft were strafed on Evere airfield. Stark's turn next, and a transport, thought to be a Caudron-Goeland at the time but now known to have been a Fw 58 of *Flugbereitschaft Ld.Kdo*, was left mangled in the back garden of a Brussels home. Finally, Detal pursued and shot down a Bf 109 of 6./JG 2, which crashed and set fire to a house in the southern suburbs of Brussels. Detal was worried that it was his own! These were Detal's fifth and sixth kills – and his last, for this talented pilot would perish in a flying accident barely two months later.

In February four more pilots would pass the five-kill mark before the Typhoon's fighter days were over. The first of these was Norman Lucas of No 266 Sqn who, with four confirmed (including three shared) already mentioned, added a fifth on 9 February during 'Rodeo 78' near Evreux.

This action was rather different from the usual full throttle pursuit, as the following report details.

Leaving its Manston dispersal is long-range Typhoon JR371 'TP-R' of No 198 Sqn. Flg Off J Macdonald shot down a Ju 88, and shared an Ar 96 with three other pilots, in this aircraft on 13 January 1944 (*via G Seager*)

Wg Cdr R T P Davidson with his unique (certainly on a Typhoon!) scoreboard showing two Japanese, two Italian and a German victory. This photograph was taken on 1 October 1943 when he had just been promoted to Wing Commander Flying No 121 Airfield, taking with him his No 175 Sqn Typhoon JP496 'HH-W'

Davidson's Typhoon JP496 (still with 'W' beneath the spinner) is seen at Lydd. By now it wore his shortened initials 'R-D', split by the roundel (*PAC*)

Lucas first saw an unidentified aircraft about five miles away to starboard, and he gave chase;

'When about 1500 yards behind e/a I recognised it as a Do.24 flying-boat, so put my rad shutter down and throttled right back. I opened fire with a three second burst from 500 yds closing to 200 from dead astern and slightly below.

'I saw strikes all over E/A, with both outer engines on fire and the "sponsons" bursting into flames, which spread along the fuselage very rapidly. F/O Miller attacked after I had broken away and as a result of his attack I saw several explosions and the flames spread along the wings.

'What was left of the E/A skimmed along a couple of fields, hit a tree, cart-wheeled and exploded. The smoke from this explosion spread to a height of about 1000 feet.'

The 'rad shutter' mentioned in this report was the hinged flap beneath the radiator fairing, which in addition to promoting cooling at lower speeds, could also be effectively used as an air brake.

No 266 Sqn was in action again the next day, and this time it was Flt Lt Johnny Deall's turn for a fifth victory. Eight Typhoons took off from Beaulieu, in the New Forest, led by Wg Cdr Baker on 10 Group's 'Rodeo 80'. Classic action followed when the Typhoons arrived at Etampes airfield, where about 15 Ju 88s were disperse;

'I attacked J.U. 88 firing a short burst from 300 - 200 yards, hitting the E/A on the fuselage between the mainplanes. The E/A burst into flames. Looking back after the attack I saw the E/A burning fiercely, flames nearly ten feet high. I claim this E/A as destroyed. We reformed and set course on 010°. Approaching another "drome" BRETIGNY, I attacked a large E/A which had landed on its belly, a DO 217 I think. The E/A was being worked on by a working party, a vehicle of sorts was standing next to this E/A. My first shell fell a little short but eventually I got strikes on the E/A, scattering the working party left and right, and probably killing a few. After this attack I saw a J.U. 88 flying west at 1,000 ft. Calling up W/C Baker I went into attack firing a 2 secs burst from 350 to 150 yds, angle of attack 20°-10°, getting large strikes all over the E/A which went up in flames, broke in half, the tail and part of the fuselage hitting the deck after the main part of the E/A. At this stage I was separated from W/Cdr Baker and his No. 2, with the remaining A/C. (2 of 266 and 1 of 193 Squadron), I set course westwards. After three minutes on this course my No. 2, F/O McGibbon, reported E/A to starboard we turned towards the E/A which were trainer (Harvard) types going into land. I was unable to get in an attack. Flying Officer McGibbon shot down three of them. Seeing no more E/A about, I told the Section to reform and set course for home.'

The 'Harvard' trainers were in fact Yales, the fixed undercarriage version of the trainer delivered to the French prior to the start of the war. McGibbon was the fourth, and last, Typhoon pilot to claim three aerial victories in a single sortie.

On 12 February Flt Lt John Niblett (one of No 198 Sqn's flight commanders) scored his fifth kill in six weeks – a LeO 45 – to add to a share in a Me 210, a Bf 109 and two Fw 190s. Within three months he would be commanding the unit.

The last of February's new aces was 'Cheval' Lallemant, although his own researches indicate that his Fw 190 'probable' had been confirmed destroyed by the 'Y' radio listening service, which would make him an ace much earlier (14 February 1943) and, indeed, the first Typhoon ace. He also destroyed a Me 210 on 21 January 1944 whilst serving with No 197 Sqn, although he was not allowed to submit a claim for this victory because his Wing Leader was annoyed that he had requested a transfer to No 198 Sqn! Lallemant later confirmed this kill for himself by locating the wreckage following the D-Day invasion.

However, his official fifth enemy aircraft destroyed was logged on 26 February when (now flying with No 198 Sqn) he and his No 2, Flg Off Hardy, unexpectedly encountered a Bf 110 nightfighter off Dunkirk following a fruitless scramble from Manston. After first attacking head on, the Typhoons whirled round to pour more cannon fire into the hapless twin-engined fighter, which plunged into the sea. The pilot was 54-victory *experte*, Oberfeldwebel Helmut Vinke of IV./NJG 1, who had made the unwise decision to fly his unwieldy nightfighter over the Channel during daylight hours.

By now the Typhoon's days as a pure fighter were well and truly numbered. Fighter Command's remaining Typhoon squadrons joined the mobile 2nd TAF Wings which were being organised, and even Nos 198 and 609 Sqns found themselves flying aircraft weighed down by rocket rails. Their independence was now gone, as road, rail and radar sites were systematically destroyed in preparation for the invasion.

One of the new units formed at this time was No 136 Wing, led by Mike Bryan, who had kept his 'hand in' with No 198 Sqn while flying a desk 'on rest'. His fifth victory – his fourth on Typhoons – had been achieved in this way on 13 January, but his fifth Typhoon kill was added on 18 May after he had joined the Wing. His shared destruction of a Bf 109 made him the last pilot to achieve 'acedom' on Typhoons. In the wake of the invasion, Typhoon pilots would claim a further 50 kills, but they would be thinly spread across 17 squadrons.

The achievements of the Typhoon pilots over the two years since operations had begun can hardly be summed up better than by one of them, Wg Cdr 'Bee' Beamont, who had done so much to start the process;

'. . . a new breed of fighter pilot had emerged. The traditional Spitfire "fighter boys" were still much in evidence and in demand for their essential work of establishing and maintaining air superiority, but the "mud-movers" of the Typhoon force, and the later Tempests, had become a rough, take-on-anything group of dedicated low-attack pilots, confident in their ability to take their massive fighters through anything the enemy, or the weather, had to offer, and to strike their targets accurately and hard with rockets, bombs, or their favourite 20 mm cannon.

'They were skilled, courageous pilots, proud of the task in which they could clearly see the results every day from "D-Day" onwards, of supporting and often saving our valiant ground forces from heavy losses in the historic drive across Europe.'

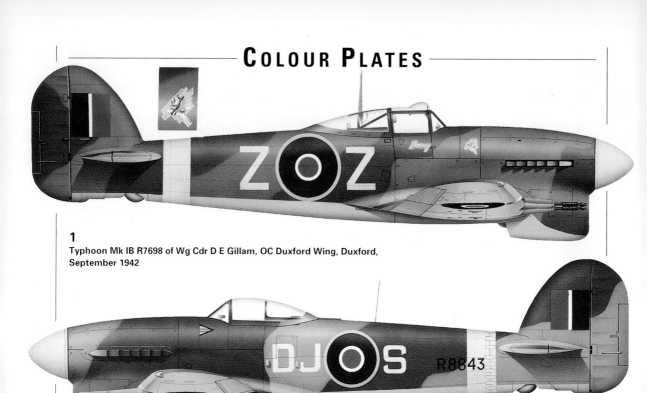

1
Typhoon Mk IB R7698 of Wg Cdr D E Gillam, OC Duxford Wing, Duxford,
September 1942

2
Typhoon Mk IB R8843 of Wg Cdr D J Scott, OC Tangmere Wing, Tangmere, September 1943

3
Typhoon Mk IB MN570 of Wg Cdr R E P Brooker, OC No 123 Wing, Thorney Island, June 1944

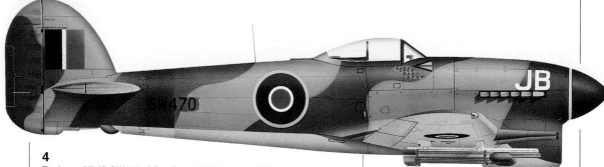

4
Typhoon Mk IB SW470 of Grp Capt J R Baldwin, OC No 123 Wing,
Plantlunne (B.103), May 1945

5
Typhoon Mk IB MN518 of Wg Cdr R T P Davidson, OC No 143 Wing, Hurn, May 1944

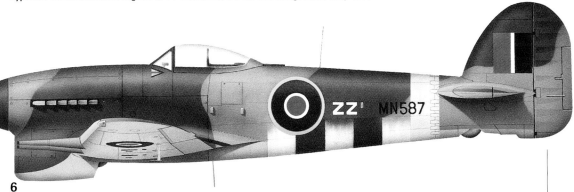

6
Typhoon Mk IB MN587 of Grp Capt D E Gillam, OC No 146 Wing, Antwerp (B.70), October 1944

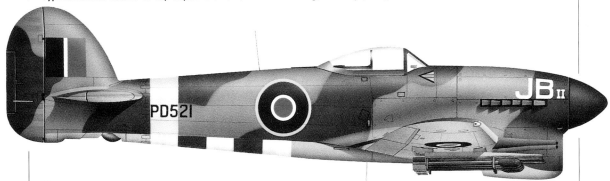

7
Typhoon Mk IB PD521 of Wg Cdr J R Baldwin, OC No 146 Wing, Antwerp (B.70), November 1944

8
Typhoon Mk IA R7648 of Sqn Ldr H S L Dundas, OC No 56 Sqn, Duxford, June 1942

9
Typhoon Mk IB MN134 of Flg Off A N Sames, No 137 Sqn, Manston, June 1944

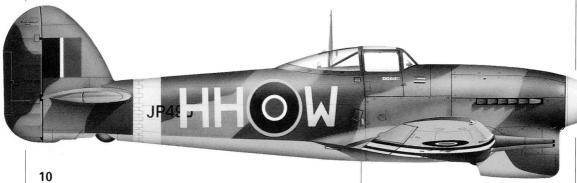

10
Typhoon Mk IB JP496 of Sqn Ldr R T P Davidson, OC No 175 Sqn, Lydd, August 1943

11
Typhoon Mk IB EK270 of Sqn Ldr D Crowley-Milling, OC No 181 Sqn, Appledram, June 1943

12
Typhoon Mk IB EK195 of Plt Off J A S Allen, No 182 Sqn, Appledram, June 1943

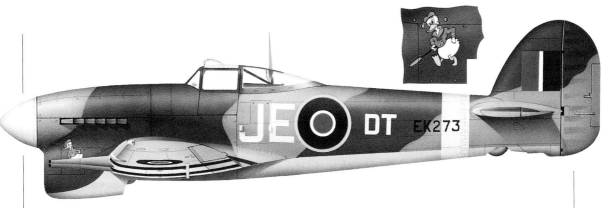

13
Typhoon Mk IB EK273 of Sqn Ldr Don 'Butch' Taylor, OC No 195 Sqn, Ludham, June 1943

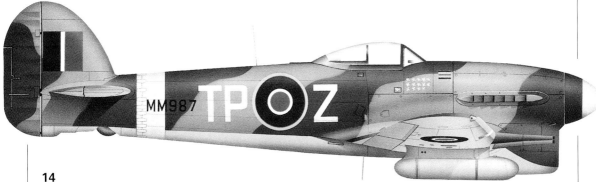

14
Typhoon Mk IB MM987 of Sqn Ldr J R Baldwin, OC No 198 Sqn, Manston, March 1944

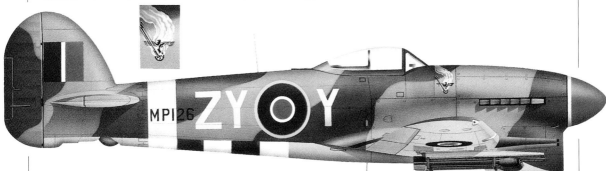

15
Typhoon Mk IB MP126 of Sqn Ldr B G Stapleton, OC No 247 Sqn, Eindhoven (B.78), December 1944

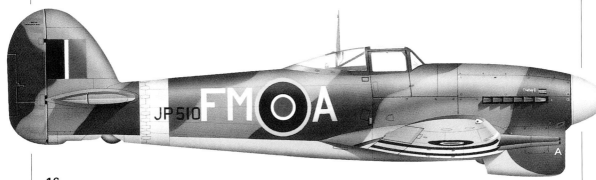

16
Typhoon Mk IB JP510 of Sqn Ldr R H Fokes, OC No 257 Sqn, Warmwell, August 1943

17
Typhoon Mk IB JP846 of Sqn Ldr P W Lefevre, OC No 266 Sqn, Harrowbeer, January 1944

18
Typhoon Mk IB JP906 of Flg Off N J Lucas, No 266 Sqn, Harrowbeer, October 1943

19
Typhoon Mk IB RB281 of Flg Off A H Fraser, No 439 Sqn,
Eindhoven (B.78), February 1945

20
Typhoon Mk IB R8781 of Sgt K G Taylor-Cannon, No 486 Sqn, Tangmere, December 1942

21
Typhoon Mk IB EJ981 of Sqn Ldr D J Scott, OC No 486 Sqn, Tangmere, June 1943

22
Typhoon Mk IB R7752 of Sqn Ldr R P Beamont, OC No 609 Sqn, Manston, February 1943

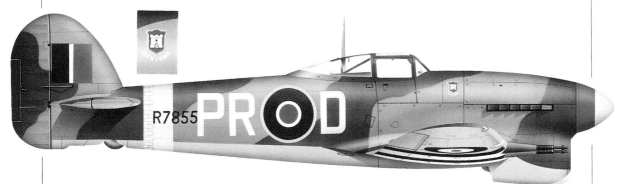

23
Typhoon Mk IB R7855 of Flg Off R A Lallemant, No 609 Sqn, Manston, February 1943

24
Typhoon Mk IB SW411 of Sqn Ldr L W F Stark, OC No 609 Sqn, Plantlunne (B.103), May 1945

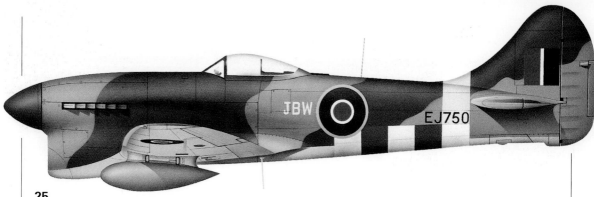

25
Tempest Mk V EJ750 of Wg Cdr Wray, OC No 122 Wing, Volkel (B.80), November 1944

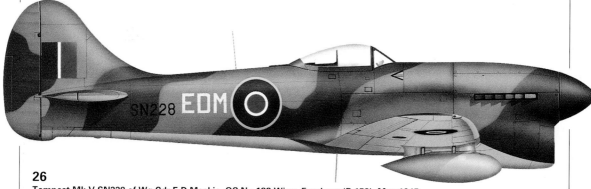

26
Tempest Mk V SN228 of Wg Cdr E D Mackie, OC No 122 Wing, Fassberg (B.152), May 1945

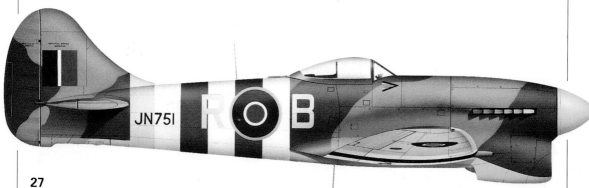

27
Tempest Mk V JN751 of Wg Cdr R P Beamont, OC No 150 Wing, Newchurch, June 1944

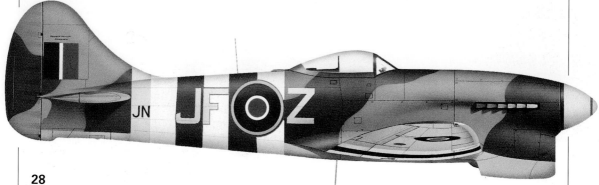

28
Tempest Mk V JN862 of Flt Lt R Van Lierde, No 3 Sqn, Newchurch, June 1944

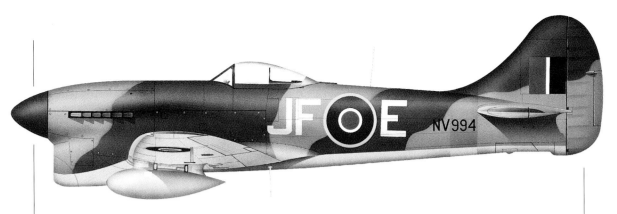

29
Tempest Mk V NV994 of Flt Lt P H Clostermann, No 3 Sqn, Hopsten (B.112), April 1945

30
Tempest Mk V EJ880 of Flt Lt L C Luckhoff, No 33 Sqn, Gilze-Rijen (B.77), February 1945

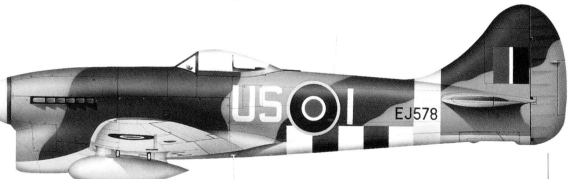

31
Tempest Mk V EJ578 of Flg Off J J Payton, No 56 Sqn, Grimbergen (B.60), September 1944

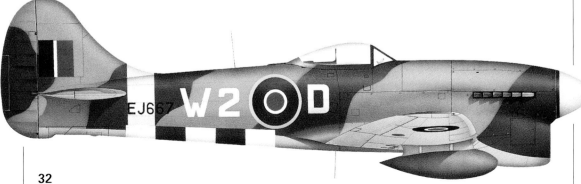

32
Tempest Mk V EJ667 of Flg Off J W Garland, No 80 Sqn, Volkel (B.80), December 1944

33
Tempest Mk V NV700 of Sqn Ldr E D Mackie, OC No 80 Sqn, Volkel (B.80), March 1945

34
Tempest Mk V NV774 of Flt Lt L McAuliffe, No 222 Sqn, Gilze-Rijen (B.77), March 1945

35
Tempest Mk V EJ762 of Flt Lt D C Fairbanks, No 274 Sqn, Volkel (B.80), November 1945

36
Tempest Mk V NV722 of Sqn Ldr W J Hibbert, OC No 274 Sqn, Volkel (B.80), March 1945

37
Tempest Mk V JN803 of Wt Off J H Stafford, No 486 Sqn, Grimbergen (B.60), September 1944

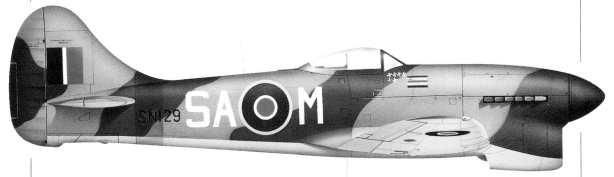

38
Tempest Mk V SN129 of Sqn Ldr C J Sheddan, OC No 486 Sqn, Fassberg (B.152), May 1945

39
Tempest Mk V NV969 of Sqn Ldr W E Schrader, OC No 486 Sqn, Hopsten (B.112), April 1945

40
Tempest Mk V EJ558 of Flg Off B F Miller (USAAF), No 501 Sqn, Bradwell Bay, October 1944

1
Sqn Ldr A E Umbers, OC No 486 Sqn, RNZAF, in early 1945

2
Wg Cdr R P Beamont, Wing Commander Flying No 150 Wing

3
Wg Cdr D J Scott, RNZAF, Tangmere Wing Leader in late 1943

4
Flg Off Hugh Fraser of No 439 Sqn,
RCAF

5
Sqn Ldr Johnny Baldwin, OC No 198
Sqn, in the winter of 1943/44

6
Sqn Ldr David Fairbanks, RCAF, OC
No 274 Sqn, in February 1945

D-DAY AND 'DIVERS'

While the Typhoon squadrons had been re-organising to support the D-Day invasion, a new 'player' entered the scene – the Hawker Tempest. As early as 1940, the limitations of the Typhoon's thick wing had been realised, and a redesign was commenced in September 1941. A new thin wing required relocation of wing fuel tanks, so the fuselage of the improved Typhoon Mk II was lengthened accordingly to allow the insertion of a 76-gallon tank forward of the cockpit. The resulting aircraft differed so much from the Typhoon that it was soon renamed 'Tempest'.

Several versions were developed with different engines, but the one with the Napier Sabre was the first to see service – perversely, this was numbered as the 'Mk V'. The Mks I, III and IV would never see service, but the Bristol Centaurus-powered Mk II would reach RAF squadrons just too late to see action in the war.

The first production Tempest V flew on 21 June 1943, being part of an initial order for 100 such aircraft. These fighters were known as the

After his successful tour of operations with No 609 Sqn, in which he had helped 'put the Typhoon on the map', 'Bee' Beamont had spent his rest tour with Hawker Aircraft helping develop the Tempest. In February 1944 he was promoted to command the first Tempest Wing, and he is seen here with his personal aircraft (*IWM CH 12767*)

That aircraft was JN751 'R-B', which was photographed at Castle Camps during the Wing's work-up period in early 1944 (*IWM CH 13959*)

Mk V Series 1, and were distinguished from later Mk V Series 2s by having the longer-barrelled Hispano Mk II cannons which protruded some eight inches beyond the leading edge of the wing.

In October of the same year, the third production Tempest V was delivered to A&AEE Boscombe Down for a series of tests which included performance and handling trials. The resultant report was generally satisfactory, with the main areas of criticism being heavy ailerons (although they could still be moved even when the fighter was flying at 535 mph IAS in a dive) and poor roll rate. These aspects would soon be greatly improved with the fitting of spring-tab ailerons.

The view from the cockpit (with a canopy identical to that of the sliding hood Typhoon) was considered excellent. Maximum speed was found to vary between 376 mph at a sea level and 432 mph at 18,400 ft, with a very useful 411 mph being recorded at a 6600 ft. It was apparent that with a little more refinement, the RAF was about to receive its most potent medium- and low-level fighter yet.

To find out just how good the Tempest was going to be, an early production aircraft was despatched to the AFDU at Wittering for comparative trials with current Allied and German fighters. By now production aircraft were fitted with the spring-tab ailerons, which dramatically improved the roll rate, especially at speeds above 250 mph IAS.

The Tempest was firstly flown against a Typhoon (with the old canopy), and the benefits offered by the former's new canopy were immediately apparent in take-off, landing, formation flying and dogfighting. The all-round view was considered superior to any Allied or enemy aircraft in service at that time. The engine was smoother and rudder, ailerons and elevators were all found to be more effective than its predecessor's. Maximum speeds at various altitudes and settings were around 15-20 mph higher than the Typhoon's, this extra speed compensating for the reduced internal fuel capacity which gave the Tempest a similar range to the Typhoon.

Climb rate was about 300 ft/min better at maximum rate of climb, but 'zoom' climb was greatly improved due to the aircraft's cleaner airframe, and dive performance similarly benefited. In fact the Tempest's

JN751 is seen again, this time after D-Day. Its immaculate 'Invasion stripes' had been applied at the Hawker factory at Langley, and make for an interesting comparison with the stripes applied 'in the field' on some of the other Newchurch Tempests. Beamont claimed the type's first air combat success in this very aircraft on 8 June 1944 (*R P Beamont*)

acceleration in the dive was remarkable – this and its steadiness as a gun platform would be the keys to its success in combat over north-west Europe.

Flights against the Mustang III, Spitfire XIV, Bf 109G and Fw 190A revealed that the Tempest was faster than all of them below 20,000 ft – 15-20 mph in the case of the Allied types, and 40-50 mph for the German aircraft. At higher levels the Mustang and Spitfire soon reversed this, but while the Bf 109G could match the Tempest, the Fw 190 remained slower.

The Tempest could just be out turned by the Mustang, and more easily by the Spitfire, but it could hold its own with the Fw 190 and out-turn the Bf 109, which was embarrassed by its leading edge slats opening near the stall. In roll rate the Tempest could not compare with the Fw 190, and was also inferior to the Mustang and the Spitfire, although the situation was reversed with the latter at speeds above 350 mph. Below this speed, the Tempest was roughly equal to the Bf 109, but above it the German fighter could be lost by making a quick change of bank and direction.

In comparing the Tempest with the Spitfire XIV, the AFDU noted that the attributes of the two aircraft were completely different, and for this reason Typhoon squadrons should re-equip with Tempests and the Spitfire XIVs should go to units equipped with earlier marks of Spitfire. This sound policy was initially followed, and the first Tempests were delivered to Nos 3 and 486 Sqns early in 1944. Delivery rates, however, were slow, and when the first Wing formed at Newchurch at he end of April 1944, these two units were joined by No 56 Sqn, which still had a few Typhoons and some stop-gap Spitfire IXs. The Wing Commander Flying was, most appropriately, none other than 'Bee' Beamont, fresh from a 'rest' tour as a test pilot with Hawker Aircraft, where he had helped develop the aircraft he would now take into operational service.

Beamont worked hard to have his Wing ready for the 'second front', and although declared operational on 7 May, the outfit was still missing Tempests for its third squadron – unbelievably, this was largely due to an industrial dispute at Hawker Aircraft. Held in reserve for most of D-Day, the Tempests were eventually called on to undertake an operation at dusk, in poor weather, only to be recalled as night set in. The next day passed uneventfully, but on D+2 action was found at last. Leading No 3 Sqn on a patrol line between Rouen and Lisieux, with No 486 Sqn as cover, Beamont spotted five Bf 109Gs in line astern some 5000 ft below. Diving down to intercept, he was able to close in behind the enemy formation, choosing the last man as his target, as he recalled in *Tempest Over Europe*;

'At about 500 yards they saw us coming and broke very sharply to port with maximum boost exhaust smoke and curling white vortices streaming from their wing tips. Eliminating consideration of the leader and the rest, I fastened on to my target and pulled tightly inside

Wg Cdr Peter Brooker had reached ace status (seven destroyed, two probables and one damaged) flying Hurricanes in the Far East. He then spent time at the Fighter Leaders School upon his return to the UK, before taking command of No 123 Wing (*via C Shores*)

Wg Cdr Brooker's Typhoon (MN570 'B') was filmed taking off from Thorney Island on D-Day (*IWM FLM 3107*)

The only casualty resulting from the first Tempest combat on 8 June 1944 was JN796 'JF-A', which suffered an over-speeding propeller. Flt Sgt M J A Rose pulled of a good forced landing within the Allied beachhead, and the Tempest was subsequently retrieved and repaired (*IWM FLM 3109*)

his turn to open fire with a short burst at about 400 yards. We were closing very fast and as he rocked his wings in violent changes of bank I had to throttle back sharply to stabilise below his tail-wheel at about 100 yards, and in an over-the-vertical bank and at about "one ring" deflection, which gave an aim line well forward and of his spinner, a second short burst showed strikes on fuselage and wing roots and he suddenly streamed smoke and oil on to my windscreen.

'Breaking right as he slowed sharply, I rolled back alongside his tailplane and saw fire streaming from the wing roots but no sign of the pilot in the cockpit.

'Confident of cover by my No 2, "Lefty" Whitman, I had not looked back for a significant few seconds, and then bang! The Tempest shook, there was a strong smell of cordite, and a cauliflower-sized hole had appeared in my starboard wing!'

'Lefty' Whitman has also written of this first Tempest combat in *Listen to Us*;

'. . . I realised that they were sucking us in and as we attacked I looked behind and here was the other pair diving down on us out of the sun. I throttled back as "Bee" fired at one of the four (sic) and yanked my Tempest into a hard turn, firing at the leader who exploded like a clay pigeon. Snap-rolling back, I saw "Bee's" target breaking up and as I tried to get the second in my sights he dived vertically into the cloud and I followed. Assuming that he would be heading east, I went down almost to the deck but couldn't find any trace of him. I heard "Bee" telling 3 Sqn to keep quiet, as there was a lot of chat, while they pursued remaining 109s. He had disappeared, having caught a cannon shell in the right wing and we both came home separately.'

'Bee' landed safely, and his Tempest, 'RB' JN751, was fitted with a new wing. The only other casualty was Flt Sgt Rose, who put his Tempest down in the beachhead area with an over-speeding propeller. Flt Lt A R Moore also destroyed a Bf 109, giving both the Wing and the Tempest an excellent start to their air combat careers. On subsequent days more patrols were made over Normandy, but the only enemy reaction encountered was in the form of flak – in due course this ever-present hazard would claim the lives of more Tempest pilots than their Luftwaffe counterparts.

Life for the Tempest Wing was about to change drastically. On the night of 12/13 June 1944, a new sound was heard over south-east England. The first of the V1 'flying bombs' had been launched in the early hours, arriving in the area south-east of London shortly after 0400. Problems at the launch sites delayed the full-scale assault until the night of 15/16 June, and the Tempest wing began patrols to intercept the new menace, code-named 'Diver', the very next morning. The battle would continue for the best part of three months, until the Allied armies overran all the potential launch sites within range of England.

The new adversary was a pilotless aircraft built by Fieseler and designated the Fi 103, but dubbed by the German propaganda machine *Vergeltungswaffen*. Later joined by the far more deadly A4 ballistic rocket, the two devices would become known as V1 and V2 respectively. To the British public they were also know as 'buzz-bombs' (after the raucous rattle of their pulse jets) or 'doodlebugs' (a nickname allegedly coined by a No 486 Sqn pilot). The V1 was a diminutive aircraft (with a wing span of less than six metres, or 19 ft), powered by an Argus pulse jet that was capable of propelling it through the air at speeds in excess of 400 mph at a height of between 1000-5000 ft.

During the first 12 days of the campaign, 2000 V1s (each carrying an 1870-lb Amatol warhead) were launched from ramps in the coastal belt of northern France, and in the weeks that followed, an average of nearly 100 per day crossed the Channel. The combination of low altitude, high speed and small size made them difficult targets to intercept, and then destroy.

Of the Allied fighter aircraft available to defend the UK against this threat, the Tempest, with its high cruising and maximum speeds at low level, was most suited to the role. The Newchurch Wing was therefore

Pilots of No 3 Sqn receive a briefing around the tail of Tempest JN812 'JF-M' at Newchurch in July 1944. The Tempest shows signs of repainting around the code letters, where they had been changed from 'QO' to 'JF' the day before D-Day (*IWM CH 18814*)

Quick turn-arounds were the order of the day at Newchurch so as to maintain the level of anti-'Diver' patrols required. On the starboard wing refuelling is taking place, while an armourer tends to the ammunition bay and an engine fitter tops up the oil (*IWM CH 14088*)

fully committed, maintaining patrols of as many pairs of aircraft as possible throughout the day and single aircraft operating throughout the night.

Although the Tempests were best suited to defeating the V1s, the sheer volume of the task meant they shared the role with Spitfire XIVs and Mustangs by day and Mosquitoes by night, whilst other types – earlier marks of Spitfire, Typhoons and, eventually, the first Meteor jet fighters – were all involved at some stage in the battle.

In the early days of the campaign it was somewhat of a 'free-for-all', which resulted in more than one aircraft attempting to intercept simultaneously, and thus impeding each others' attacks. Frustrated pilots able only to close the range slowly, sometimes pursued the bombs to the Capital, whilst anti-aircraft gunners, equally determined to bring down the intruding 'Divers', opened fire, endangering the fighters.

Soon, the defences were organised into three bands – first line was the fighter patrols which took place over the Channel; second line was the anti-aircraft guns, in a wide arc between the coast and London; and the final defence were the barrage balloons on the outskirts of London.

By day, the technique developed by fighter pilots was to patrol at 3000 ft above the incoming 'Divers', awaiting radar vectors to achieve interceptions. The average speed of the bombs was around 400 mph, but some were faster and some slower. The Tempests were positioned so as to overhaul their targets in a shallow dive in a stern chase, and as the bombs presented small targets, pilots usually closed to a short range before opening fire in order to improve their chance of success.

This technique involved considerable risk, for when the bomb and its warhead exploded, the pursuing fighter would have no chance of avoiding the conflagration. The pilots were little comforted by the thought that by piercing the centre of the explosion, the majority of the debris would have already cleared their path. Two Tempests were lost through this cause (one with its pilot) and many others were damaged.

The subject of one of the most famous Tempest photos ever taken, the identity of No 3 Sqn's 'JF-Z' has, until recently, remained a mystery. However, new research has revealed the aircraft to be JN862, flown by 'B' Flight commander, Flt Lt 'Mony' Van Lierde. A highly skilled pilot, Van Lierde was the ranking V1 ace by day, destroying 44 flying bombs. Close examination of the original print has shown that the stripe round the spinner is in fact three narrow bands – in view of Van Lierde's origins, these were quite likely to have been applied in Belgian national colours (*IWM CH 14095*)

To reinforce the night defences, a detachment from the Fighter Interception Unit (FIU) arrived at Newchurch with a handful of Tempests and pilots, the latter having experience on Beaufighter or Mosquito nightfighters. Like the day fighter pilots, these nocturnal hunters had their successes too, with Flt Lt Joe Berry in particular demonstrating his skill at this arcane art, night after night. By 7 August his score had reached an incredible 52 and 1 shared – he had destroyed seven of these on one night!

At this point the FIU pilots were posted to Manston to be amalgamated with No 501 Sqn, which had just equipped with Tempests. Berry was promoted to take command, and continuing the success of the FIU at night, his score reached 60 (including 1 shared). Tragically, he was shot down and killed by flak on 2 October 1944 whilst leading three Tempests

After flying Tempests for most of the anti-'Diver' campaign, Van Lierde was promoted to command No 164 Sqn, eqipped with rocket-Typhoons. He is seen here meeting General Eisenhower at Gilze-Rijen during his visit to No 123 Wing in November 1944 (*RNZAF*)

on a 'Ranger' over Holland. This was only the second such mission No 501 Sqn had undertaken since swapping its Spitfire IXs for Tempest Vs.

As the battle progressed more hazards became evident. The very pace of the round-the-clock patrols induced fatigue, and mistakes were made. Competing fighters baulked each others' attacks and even collided – Tempests were lost in mid-air collisions with a Spitfire and a Mosquito. 'Friendly flak' was also responsible for two Tempests being destroyed and many damaged, whilst several pilots were killed in crashes during bad weather or at

night. Other Tempests were lost through engine failure, for although the Sabre engine was now acceptably reliable, operations at constant high throttle settings were taking their toll. One of the pilots lost to this cause was Sqn Ldr E G Daniel (seven destroyed, one damaged and four V1s destroyed) of the FIU, who had flown Beaufighter nightfighters in Malta two years earlier.

But the campaign continued, and not a day passed without the Newchurch Wing making claims. Its pilots began to build up impressive scores, and foremost among them was the previously successful Typhoon ace, Flt Lt 'Mony' Van Lierde, now commanding No 3 Sqn's 'B' flight. On 23 June alone, he destroyed no less than five 'Divers' in a single day, and by the end of the campaign his total had reached 44, making him the top scorer by day.

Wg Cdr 'Bee' Beamont's contribution was not only 31 flying bombs destroyed, but also the refinement of Tempest tactics, which he recalled as follows;

'There was the question of firing range and how close to go in, relative to the chances of blowing yourself up when the warhead exploded. Starting at 400 yards we experienced much wastage and frequent missing altogether until, when closing to 200 yards before firing, a higher success rate was achieved but losses were sustained due to debris and fire damage. I was convinced that the standard Fighter Command "spread harmonisation" pattern for the guns was unsuitable for this operation and, after failing to obtain official approval, had my own guns point-harmonised at 300

Flt Sgt Owen Eagleson uses one of the retractable footsteps to descend from the cockpit of Tempest JN854 'SA-G' whilst simultaneously indicating success to the awaiting audience. Although this may be a posed publicity shot, Eagleson did shoot down a V1 in this aircraft on 28 June 1944, and went on to become No 486 Sqn's top scorer against flying bombs, with 23 destroyed (including 3 shares). 'SA-G' (in the hands of various pilots) was responsible for the destruction of 15 bombs (*IWM CH 18170*)

Flt Sgt R W Cole, who was one of No 3 Sqn's most successful V1 'killers' (24 destroyed, including 4 shares), examines the damage to his Tempest after flying through an exploding 'Diver'. Fabric surfaces and paintwork could suffer badly in the heat of the explosion, but the real danger was from debris – especially threatening to the Tempest's prominent radiator (*IWM CH 13401*)

yards. This had an immediate effect for the better on my shooting and I was able to hit the next lot of V1s with my first burst and with good effect. Accordingly I ordered all 150 Wing guns point-harmonised in disregard of Command policy with two results: the first, an immediate and sustained improvement on the Wing's scoring rate, and the second, not unexpectedly, was a different sort of rocket from headquarters!'

Another technique was developed for use by day. Frustrated pilots closing on a 'Diver' only to find they were out of ammunition, discovered that it was possible to draw alongside and edge their fighter's wing under that of the flying bomb. All (!) that was then required was the nerve to flick their own aircraft's wing smartly upwards – the sudden disruption to the V1's progress was usually enough to topple the gyros and cause it to crash.

Plt Off G A 'Lefty' Whitman is seen climbing out of Tempest JN807 'JF-X' of No 3 Sqn at Newcurch in late June 1944. Whitman, an American serving in the RCAF, was Beamont's No 2 in the first Tempest air combat, and during the sortie he destroyed a Bf 109G which was intent on attacking his leader. He was flying JN743 'JF-P' on that occasion (*IWM CH 14092*)

Beamont's No 2, 'Lefty' Whitman, came to the end of his tour before the V1 campaign was over, and recalls his last sortie;

'Just as I turned over Goodwin Sands, tracers criss-crossed the estuary, tracking the course of my target. It was at about 1000 ft, just visible above the fog banks. Starting off at full throttle, I was quickly in a firing position, but not a moment too soon. There, directly in front, was the balloon fence. A short burst blew number fourteen to smithereens; another few seconds and the Battersea power station would likely have been hit as it lay dead ahead. As I circled to report my "kill", people rushed out of the row of houses, waving, and I knew that my victory roll would help keep the morale up.'

As the above passage indicates, 'Lefty' Whitman claimed 14 bombs destroyed (7 solo victories and 7 shared), yet 'official records' indicate he was credited with '5 and 5 shared'. Many pilots involved feel their claims were unfairly adjusted, and 'Lefty' has this to say;

'It was a combination of luck, plus some "claim jumping", that translated into high scores and high decorations for those who practised the art. Claims were constantly being readjusted at squadron level, and, as I was to discover later, at Command level as well. The "guns"

New Zealander 'Spike' Umbers had completed a tour with No 486 Sqn before joining No 3 Sqn as a flight commander. He claimed 18 V1s destroyed, and later returned to No 486 Sqn as CO, reaching ace status in January 1945. He was shot down by flak and killed on a last, impromptu, sortie, when the aircraft due to take him back to the UK was delayed (*IWM CH 13403*)

were occasionally given credit for "kills" for morale boosting and, we suspected, for boosting of other sorts. It was not unusual to discover that you had been given a half credit, or one quarter, or some other fraction of a "kill" that you thought you had made alone.'

In light of the above, the listing of V1 claims in Appendix IV, which is based on the official records, should be viewed as the most accurate possible under confused circumstances. Whatever individual scores were, the fact remains that the Tempest pilots were the most successful of the intercepting fighters. Again, exact scores are difficult to pin down as sources vary, but the lowest totals quoted for the Newchurch Wing are: No 3 Sqn, 288; No 486 Sqn, 239$\frac{1}{2}$; and No 56 Sqn, 70$\frac{1}{2}$ (one of the these was by a Spitfire prior to the first Tempests being received). To these figures must be added the Wing Commander's own tally of 31. Also at Newchurch was the FIU detachment, with claims totalling 86$\frac{1}{2}$, all but two of which were scored at night. The Manston-based Tempest units, Nos 274 and 501 Sqns, scored 15 and 88 respectively (the latter including claims up to March 1945), making a grand total well in excess of 800 – more than all the other fighter types put together.

In direct comparison with the three-squadron Newchurch Wing (two-squadron for much of the period, as No 56 Sqn did not fly its first Tempest sortie until 2 July), whose total score was in excess of 620, the three Spitfire XIV squadrons committed to the anti-'Diver' campaign were responsible for the destruction of approximately 340 V1s.

As a footnote to the success of the

Tempest JN803 'SA-D' was occasionally flown by No 486 Sqn's Owen Eagleson. Seen in late September 1944, this aircraft sports a scoreboard (just visible on the original print underneath what appears to be a discarded flying jacket) comprising plan silhouettes of 'Divers' destroyed by its numerous pilots (*Eagleson via A Cranston*)

Top V1 ace, Sqn Ldr Joseph Berry destroyed no less than 60 'buzz-bombs', most of which were claimed at night while flying with the Tempest flight of the Fighter Interception Unit – this tally included an impressive seven in one night. On 16 August 1944, Berry and 5 other FIU pilots transferred to No 501 Sqn at Manston to convert the unit onto the 'Diver' night interception role, the former also taking command of the unit. On 2 October 1944 Berry led three other Tempests on a sortie to attack airfields in Holland but was hit by flak and crashed in flames (*via N Franks*)

Tempest, the contribution made by its predecessor, the Typhoon, should not be ignored. Only one unit was involved, No 137 Sqn based at Manston. This was one of only two Typhoon units remaining under ADGB control – Air Defence of Great Britain had replaced Fighter Command when 2nd TAF was formed. The primary role of both units was anti-shipping – sealing off the invasion area from German surface raiders – but No 137 Sqn sought and gained permission to undertake anti-'Diver' sorties, provided their responsibilities were not compromised.

Between 22 June and 4 August the unit knocked down 30 bombs, with Flg Off 'Arty' Sames (already mentioned as a successful No 486 Sqn Typhoon pilot) claiming five. Another squadron pilot, Australian John Horne, attempted to catch one while still carrying his rockets after an uneventful shipping reconnaissance. Unable to close to effective cannon range, Horne lifted the nose of his Typhoon and launched four pairs of rockets at his tiny quarry. At least one of the impromptu weapons hit the 'buzz-bomb', which broke up and spun down into a field. This led to the

Three of No 501 Sqn's nocturnal V1 hunting Tempests are seen off the Essex coast in October 1944. They are EJ763 'SD-X', EJ599 'SD-W' and EJ589 'SD-J'. Note that the squadron code 'SD' is positioned ahead of the roundel, which was relatively unusual on the starboard side of Tempests (*Aeroplane*)

rapid trial of 'Z battery' rockets, complete with proximity fuses, in place of the standard rockets. And although successful on one occasion, the device was not adopted.

As mentioned earlier, the rest of the Typhoon squadrons were now under 2nd TAF control. After campaigns against the 'Noball' sites, followed by German coastal radars, these units where then fully employed in support of the invasion. Among the Wing Leaders were two aces – Wg Cdrs Mike Bryan, mentioned earlier, and Peter Brooker (seven destroyed, two probables and one damaged), who had flown Hurricanes both with No 56 Sqn in the Battle of Britain and Nos 232 and 242 Sqns in the East Indies. A third ace, Wg Cdr R T P Davidson, had commanded the new RCAF Typhoon Wing until shortly before the invasion, but had suffered engine failure over France and was now fighting with the *Maquis*. He had been replaced by Wg Cdr Mike Judd, a successful No 250 Sqn Kittyhawk pilot with four (or possibly five) victories.

Between D-Day and VE-Day, German flak would demonstrate in no uncertain way that it had little respect for flying skills, taking a steady toll of experienced pilots. Denis Sweeting, who flew with No 198 Sqn during this period, recalled some of the losses in his autobiography *Wings of Chance*. Sqn Ldr John Niblett was leading an attack on a coastal radar station four days before D-Day;

'When we were nearly a mile from the cliffs I did another check of the sight and firing guns and tightened my seat belt. The top of the radar arrays were now clearly visible, some being set on concrete emplacements just back from the cliff edge and others further inland.

'I looked towards "Nibby's" aircraft which was in front about 50 yards away, and we were now climbing to clear the 200-ft high cliffs. As I did so there was a flash under his wings, as if he had fired his rockets which I thought was too early as we were not yet within range. Then, petrified with horror, I realised that his aircraft had been hit and had burst into flames. In a split second all that became visible of the aircraft was its wing tips and tail sticking out of a ball of fire. The tips turned slowly over and the aircraft must have been on its back when it exploded into the sea.'

Filmed at Bradwell Bay on 15 October 1944 (a day when the press were invited to view Britain's defenders against air-launched V1s), Tempest V EJ558 'SD-R' was normally flown by Flg Off B F Miller. 'Bud' Miller was a USAAF exchange pilot, and had claimed his first V1 with No 605 Sqn in a Mosquito. His remaining 'Diver' kills were in Tempests, two of which came with the Fighter Interception Unit and five (possibly six) with No 501 Sqn, which he joined early in August 1944 (*IWM FLM 3111*)

Dusk at Bradwell Bay in October 1944, and Tempest EJ608 'SD-P' is prepared for a night sortie (*Aeroplane*)

Before Niblett, Mike Bryan had been No 198 Sqn's CO, and had been promoted to lead No 136 Wing, as noted earlier. Sweeting continues;

'We heard that evening that Mike Bryan, our ex-CO, had been shot down in flames leading his wing in an attack south of Caen. He had not jettisoned his long range tanks before diving and it was these that caught fire when the aircraft was hit. "Men who disobey orders expect to be killed", the Group Captain said grimly.'

Sqn Ldr I J 'Dave' Davies, who was also mentioned earlier in this volume when he claimed three kills in a single sortie with No 609 Sqn, replaced Niblett;

'The squadron went off to give close support to US troops in the Cherbourg Peninsula. A gun position, road and rail transport were attacked with good results. "Dave" Davies, seen to be hit by flak, tried to glide to the American lines. When realising he was not going to reach them, he baled out very low and his parachute did not open. He had been our CO for two momentous weeks, and had shown himself to be an inspiring and capable leader.'

Whilst the Typhoons braved the flak and got on with their essential job of ground support, they were protected from the attentions of the Luftwaffe by screens of Allied fighters. For the most part this protection was effective, but sometimes the Fw 190s or Bf 109s broke through and caught the ground attack pilots by surprise. Occasionally the Typhoons were able to fight back, though hampered in most cases by rocket rails. The dive-bombers had an advantage here, as once their bombs had gone, the racks had little adverse effect on performance.

During two of these battles Wg Cdr Baldwin was able to add three more destroyed (see Chapter Seven) to his score, bringing his final total to 15 and 1 shared destroyed and 4 damaged – more than twice that of any other Typhoon pilot. A further 13 Luftwaffe aircraft were credited to Typhoon pilots during the Normandy campaign, but in return at least 17 of their number were lost to enemy aircraft – the latter total could very well be higher, as several Luftwaffe claims may have been put down to flak or unknown causes.

HOLLAND

As the V1 launching areas were overrun by Allied troops, and the 'buzz bomb' threat dwindled to the reduced numbers launched by He 111s over the North Sea, the Newchurch Tempest Wing was at last free to join the rest of the 2nd TAF on the Continent. The Tempests flew to Grimbergen (B.60) at the end of September 1944, exchanging places in No 122 Wing with the resident Mustang squadrons. Three days later they moved forward to Volkel (B.80), in Holland. This base would be 'home' for the next six months.

The Manston Wing (Nos 80 and 274 Sqns), after short stays at Coltishall, Antwerp and Grave, also joined No 122 Wing at Volkel, thus making it a five-squadron Wing. Meanwhile, No 56 Sqn had already been in action, on 29 September, claiming three Fw 190s destroyed and a probable. Among the claimants were Flg Offs Dave Ness and Jim Payton, who would go on to be numbered among the most successful Tempest pilots of the war.

Finally, Flt Lt A R Moore, who had scored one of the Tempest Wing's first kills soon after D-Day, claimed the third victory on the 29th, thus doubling his score – he had been one of the most successful pilots during the V1 period, being credited with 24 destroyed. Unfortunately, 'his' Fw 190 claim was later downgraded to a probable and shared with another pilot. Had this not happened, he would have been on his way to becoming the first Tempest ace. As it was, he finished the war with four kills.

The Tempests were soon in action again when, on 2 October, Wg Cdr Beamont led No 56 Sqn on the first patrol from their new base. Flying over the Nijmegan area under radar control, Beamont was informed of 'trade' approaching at the same height, but in the opposite direction. The action came swiftly, as described in *Tempest Over Europe*;

'As I called, "Tally-ho, 190s straight ahead port side, breaking left after them", the leaders streamed white smoke as they opened fire apparently at the left of our formation.

Home for No 122 Wing Tempests for six months was B.80 airfield – Volkel, in Holland. Already badly damaged by USAAF bombing, destruction of the facilities was completed by the Luftwaffe before they left, under threat from the Allied advance. These Tempests are from No 3 Sqn, and they have been dispersed among the ruins. With little shelter on offer, the aircraft have had their canopies protected from the elements by tailored covers. The Tempest in the background also has a close-fitting engine cover, which was essential in order to keep the Sabre engine as warm as possible so as to aid starting in cold conditions (*IWM CL 1418*)

Sqn Ldr Bob Spurdle and Flt L J Friend walk out to their No 80 Sqn Tempests at Volkel in October 1944. Spurdle was unable to add to his score (achieved flying Spitfires with Nos 74 and 91 Sqns, and Kittyhawks with 16 Sqn RNZAF) during his period commanding this unit (*IWM CL 1393*)

Canadian Flg Off David Ness (five and one shared destroyed, plus five V1s destroyed) was one of No 56 Sqn's most successful Tempest pilots, winning a DFC in January 1945 (*via R V Dennis*)

'They missed and were already streaming past our port side when the leader rolled sharply right into a near vertical dive followed one by one by all his gang. He was presenting the Tempests with a perfect target as we had all the advantage of speed in our dive capability! I was already rolling left and pulling down towards them and, with gun-sight switched on and range bar already set for a 30 ft span at 200 yds, I called, "Down after them – balls out!"

'I had selected the nearest 190 in the weaving gaggle ahead, and there was another just off my right wing tip and falling behind fast, apparently hell-bent after the others and not bothered about me. At least I just hoped my No 2 would deal with him if he tried to get in a shot at me.

'In this near vertical dive we were already down through 7000 ft and I was catching when I fired a short burst at my target from about 300 yds. Hits and smoke from his wing roots were seen at once and the 190 nosed over to beyond the vertical. At well over 500 mph indicated I rolled easily clearing to the right, and pulled up hard, as the fields and trees now seen through the scattered cloud rushing up from below looked altogether too close at this dive angle and speed – and there below and to port was a flash and eruption of smoke and the white globe of shock wave as the 190 went straight in near Cleve. My No 2 confirmed this and said, "We were over 510 when you fired at him!"'

JETS!

Early in October, Wg Cdr John Wray arrived from Coltishall to replace Beamont, who was approaching 'tour expired'. Wray had no air combat credits to his name, despite vast experience of fighter operations flying Beaufighters, Whirlwinds, Hurricanes and Typhoons, but would soon have a couple of spectacular kills to 'break his duck'. Beamont, meanwhile, was reluctant to leave just as his Tempest squadrons were getting their teeth into the opposition. A pattern of regular patrols over the battlefield and armed reconnaissance missions deep into German territory, searching for 'targets of opportunity', was now developing. Already the Tempests had encountered Me 262 jets, but had been unable to engage.

Leading Nos 3 and 80 Sqns on an 'armed recce' on 12 October, Beamont's take-off was delayed by a bombing attack on the airfield, carried out by a lone Me 262. This would become a regular occurrence, with the Tempests making frequent return visits to the Me 262's base at Rheine in an effort to catch the jets as they slowed for landing, short of fuel for combat. The technique became known as 'Rat-catching'. Beamont would not get chance to lead the Tempests in a return visit this day – or at all – for when attacking a heavily defended troop train his Tempest streamed smoke, indicating coolant loss, and he was obliged to crash land in enemy territory, spending the rest of the war as a PoW.

The first Me 262 to be destroyed fell to Plt Off Bob Cole of No 3 Sqn on 13 October. At first unable to catch the jet in a shallow dive at 480 mph, Cole eventually managed to close the range when the Me 262 slowed, possibly due to a shortage of fuel. He swiftly despatched the enemy aircraft with a burst from 100 yards. The jets remained elusive, however, although several were claimed as damaged over the next few weeks. On 3 November John Wray's chance arrived;

'I was flying at about 18,000 ft, when I sighted two Me 262s flying in a south-westerly direction and camouflaged blue/grey. They saw me and turned in a wide arc to port, then set off in an easterly direction. I had already launched an attack, opening to full throttle and diving. My speed was in the region of 500 mph.

'I closed to about three hundred yards on the starboard aircraft and opened fire, firing about a four-second burst and hitting the tailplane. The Me 262 continued on course and started to pull away, but before he got out of range I fired again.

Suddenly a large piece flew off the aircraft and he flicked over onto his back and disappeared downwards into cloud in an inverted position. I followed, but the thickness of the cloud made it impossible for me to maintain contact.'

Wray's claim for a 'probable' was later downgraded to a 'damaged', but postwar research shows that the Me 262 was actually shot down. The jet, from *Kommando Nowotny*, crashed near Hittfeld, killing the pilot, Oberfeldwebel Willi Banzhaff.

Throughout November the Luftwaffe remained elusive, although on 26 November Flt Lt 'Hyphen' Taylor-Cannon shared a Ju 188 destroyed with another No 486 Sqn pilot and, two days later, Flt Lt A R Moore had a rare encounter with a pair of He 219s. They were soon overhauled and one, taking no evasive action, was quickly shot down. The second He 219 was also attacked and hit, but escaped into cloud and could only be claimed as a 'probable', which was later downgraded to 'damaged'. The nightfighters were from I./NJG 1.

In December the pace really began to hot up, particularly after the middle of the month when the Germans launched their Ardennes offensive. No less than 38 enemy aircraft were claimed destroyed in the air by Tempests during this month, the first, on the 3 December, being another Me 262, which was claimed by Canadian, Flg Off John 'Judy' Garland, of No 80 Sqn.

On 14 December Flt Lt Dave Ness, another Canadian, was able to

Much repair work on the damaged Dutch airfields was undertaken by local labour, who laid thousands of bricks to form taxyways, dispersals and even runways. In the background a Tempest (believed to be 'H'of No 3 Sqn, EJ or JN817) receives attention (*IWM CL1415*)

Left and below
In October 1944 Wg Cdr John Wray replaced 'Bee' Beamont as Wing Commander Flying No 122 Wing, adopting Tempest EJ750 as his aircraft and marking it, rather discretely, with his initials. He destroyed two Me 262 in this aircraft, although one was only credited as damaged (*J B Wray*)

One of eight Typhoon squadrons occupying Eindhoven (B.78) in the winter of 1944/45 was No 137 Sqn. Amongst the unit's complement of aircraft was anti-'Diver' veteran MN134 'SF-S', which was the top V1 'killing' Typhoon on No 137 Sqn. Its appearance has changed somewhat since the previous July, with the 'Invasion stripes' having been removed from the upper surfaces, its spinner painted red and the exhaust fairing removed. Note the letters 'SS' painted on the nearest rocket rail, indicating that the store should be fitted beneath the starboard wing of aircraft 'S'. A fire extinguisher (essential when starting Sabre engines) can also be seen dangling from the starboard inner cannon barrel (*AWM*)

One of the rocket-Typhoon units at Eindhoven was No 247 Sqn, commanded by Battle of Britain ace B G 'Stapme' Stapleton (six and two shared destroyed, eight probables and two damaged). He had enjoyed a lengthy career on fighters, flying Spitfires with No 603 Sqn, catapult-Hurricanes with the Merchant Ship Fighter Unit and conventional Hurricanes, and then Tempests, with No 257 Sqn, before acquiring his own command. He would finish the war in *Stalag Luft II*, having force-landed in enemy territory on 23 December 1944 following debris damage to his Typhoon from a rocket attack on a train (*F K Wiersum*)

add to his score when eight No 56 Sqn Tempests ran into four Bf 109s. He destroyed one in the initial attack, for his third victory, and his colleagues shot down two more, one of them being credited to Plt Off 'Artie' Shaw (a second Bf 109 to add to the one he had claimed three days earlier). Ness, out of ammunition and in a turning contest with the fourth Bf 109, had cause to appreciate the low-level performance of the Tempest;

'The 109 turned with me & in 3 complete turns I was not able to gain any advantage, although my a/c was on the verge of stalling at about 50 ft above the ground. I called up for assistance but due to the haze, could not be seen. I eased out of the turn, dived right down to zero feet & commenced hedge-hopping and weaving. By flying over trees and high tension wires I was able to prevent the Hun from obtaining an accurate sight of me. During the first part of the chase the 109 was able to close the range because of his more rapid acceleration, but as my A/C gained speed I pulled out of range gradually. The chase went on for 15-20 miles before I was able to climb. By then the Hun was 1000 yards or more behind me.'

On 17 December a new name appeared on the Tempest victory list – Flt Lt David Fairbanks, a US citizen flying with the RCAF. He opened his score on Tempests (he had one destroyed already, which he had claimed while flying Spitfire VBs with No 501 Sqn) in a spectacular manner with two Bf 109s destroyed and one damaged (see Chapter Seven). From this point onwards his name would appear with increasing frequency in the 2nd TAF Log of Casualty Claims, Assessment and Losses.

On the same day Flt Lt A R Moore added two Bf 109s destroyed (one of them shared) to his earlier successes. This would have brought his score to five had not his claim on 29 September been reduced to a probable. His tour would end before he had a chance to log a fifth confirmed victory.

On the same sortie Plt Off 'Artie' Ross added two shared claims – a Bf 109 and a He 219, again from I./NJG 1 – to bring his score to four.

Although many of the 2nd TAF pilots were experienced on Typhoons or Spitfires before converting to Tempests, few had previously achieved ace status. Two notable exceptions were the consecutive Commanding Officers of No 80 Sqn. Kiwi, Sqn Leader Bob Spurdle, had flown with Nos 74 and 91 Sqns in the Battle of Britain and over the Channel in 1941-42, then returned to the RNZAF in 1943 to

Groundcrew at Volkel had to cope with appalling conditions during the winter of 1944/45. In the background is Tempest V EJ548 'US-G' of No 56 Sqn, which was normally flown by Plt Off H Shaw – he used this aircraft to claim all five of his victories, making him the first Tempest ace in the process. Flg Off Jim Payton (six destroyed and one probable) achieved his third kill in this aircraft. The well-used fighter was finally lost on 16 January 1945 when it was hit by debris whilst ground strafing. Plt Off Shaw was again at the controls on this occasion, and he spent the remaining months of the war as a PoW (*IWM CL 1676*)

fly Kittyhawks with No 16 Sqn in the Solomon Islands. Here, he claimed a 'Hamp' and a 'Zeke' to bring his score to ten destroyed, two and one shared probable and nine and two shared damaged. He joined No 80 Sqn as their CO late in July 1944, and converted them from Spitfire IXs to Tempests a month later. In his autobiography, *The Blue Arena*, he enthused about the unit's new aircraft;

'Our Tempests arrived! Brand-new; shining in the sun! They seemed huge after our dainty Spitfires. But could they go! We found they cruised at almost 100 mph faster than the Spits, climbed like rockets and dived at incredible speeds. They were magnificent gun platforms and, apart from a slight tendency to swing on take-off, had no real vices. We were delighted.'

Spurdle flew 48 operational sorties on Tempests before being declared 'tour expired', and despite being very active, and successful, against ground targets, was unable to add to his score. He did, however, come near on 18 December;

'An armed recce near Bielefeld and we had a ball knocking off three locos and their wagons, then two tractor and trailer units, and a RDF station and barracks, finishing off with blowing holes in a factory roof. Four Fw 190s – the new long-nosed jobs in orbit at Bielefeld! I got behind

After converting from Spitfires to Tempests at Predannack, in Cornwall, No 33 Sqn rejoined No 135 Wing at Gilze-Rijen on 21 February 1945. This photo of the unit's Tempest V EJ880 '5R-R' was probably taken at Predannack during conversion, as the last remnants of the 'Invasion stripes' were removed from 2nd TAF aircraft early in January 1945. Note the oversized code letters favoured by both No 33 Sqn and the other Tempest unit within No 135 Wing, No 222 Sqn (*No 33 Sqn records*)

Three New Zealanders with extensive experience on Typhoons and Tempests. They are, from left to right, Harvey Sweetman (one and two shared destroyed, one and one shared probable and two and one shared damaged), 'Spike' Umbers (four and one shared destroyed, one and one shared probable and two and one shared damaged) and 'Hyphen' Taylor-Cannon (four and one shared destroyed and one shared probable). Only Sweetman, who finished his second tour as CO of No 3 Sqn, survived the war, both Umbers and Taylor-Cannon losing their lives while leading No 486 Sqn RNZAF. In this photo they are seen holding the centreboard from the airborne lifeboat which figured in the action of 15 July 1943 (see Chapter Three), and was subsequently used as the squadron scoreboard (*RNZAF*)

Flg Off Hugh Fraser of No 439 Sqn had destroyed two Fw 190s (one of them a 'Dora') before shooting down an Me 262 on 14 February 1945. He is seen here in his appropriately marked Typhoon, RB281 '5V-X' *Nicky*, which he was flying when he made his claims (*PAC*)

one as it came in to land and pressed the gun button again and again in a fury of frustration. Out of ammo! Beside myself with rage, completely irrational, I tried to ram it in the tail unit with my wing tip. Just as we were about to collide, the Hun put his flaps down and the 190 humped up and I passed beneath it, collecting two gashes from his propeller in my starboard wing tip. The Jerry must have had a fearful fright.'

In December Sqn Ldr Evan 'Rosie' Mackie, another New Zealander, arrived at Volkel, initially flying sorties with Nos 3 and 274 Sqns, before taking over command of No 80 Sqn from Spurdle early in the New Year. He was an established Spitfire ace whose score stood at 15 and 2 shared destroyed, 2 probable and 7 and 1 shared damaged (mostly gained during a tour with No 243 Sqn in North Africa and Sicily).

His first successful combat in a Tempest came quickly. On Christmas Eve 1944, while still flying as a supernumerary with No 274 Sqn, he spotted a Typhoon formation well below him under attack by a Fw 190. Diving hard, he pulled up under the Focke-Wulf, which immediately climbed, only to be overhauled by the Tempest. Mackie just had time for a two-and-a-half-second burst before he spun away at the top of his zoom climb, but it was enough, and as Mackie recovered his Tempest, the other No 274 Sqn pilots saw the Fw 190 drop a wing and spin into the ground near Eindhoven. It seems that the Fw 190 pilot was Hauptmann Wolfgang Kosse, *Staffelkapitän* of 13./JG 3, and the No 440 Sqn Typhoons he had just shot down were his 27th and 28th – and last – victories.

A third established ace who joined the ranks of Tempest pilots at this time was Flg Off Basilios Vassiliades, a 'millionaire playboy' of Greek parents, posted to No 3 Sqn. He had a enjoyed a successful spell with No 19 Sqn flying Mustang IIIs until shot down by flak in August 1944. Vassiliades had evaded capture, however, and he arrived at Volkel with a score of five and two shared destroyed and one probable. He would add three Fw 190s destroyed and a further one damaged to this total before falling to that anonymous victor over so many Typhoon and Tempest pilots – flak – on 25 March 1945.

On Christmas Day 1944, the fifth Me 262 to fall to Tempests was intercepted by No 486 Sqn. The jet was crippled in an unusual head-on attack, during which pieces were seen to fall from its port engine

Hugh Fraser's Typhoon RB281 was replaced, following an engine failure and wheels-up landing on 2 March 1945, by a new '5V-X', RB262. Hit by flak on 24 March, RB262 was in turn replaced by EK219, which was also an 'X', as shown here. A March 1943 production Typhoon, it was brought up to the latest standards (four-blade propeller, sliding hood and Tempest tailplane) prior to redelivery to the RAF in September 1944. It served with Nos 168 and 438 Sqns prior to its allocation to No 439 Sqn (*A H Fraser*)

whilst under fire from Flg Off Jack Stafford. The Tempests pursued the jet, which showed a remarkable turn of speed despite the damage, but the German pilot was forced to abandon his aircraft when it became unstable. Stafford shared this victory – his first – with another pilot.

On 27 December No 486 Sqn's 'B' Flight commander, Flt Lt Taylor-Cannon, was leading eight Tempests on an 'armed recce' when he was directed to Munster by 'Kenway'. The New Zealanders sighted two 15-aircraft formations of German fighters, which they identified as Fw 190s and Bf 109s. Taylor-Cannon led one section in to attack the formation below, whilst ordering the other section to attack the formation above. In fact, there were 60 Luftwaffe fighters in the vicinity, all of them Fw 190D-9s of III./JG 54, which had just returned to the front after re-equipment – many of the German pilots were flying their first combat mission.

Taking advantage of their greater experience, the Tempest pilots were able to claim four Focke-Wulfs destroyed, whilst a further one was credited as a probable. In fact III./JG 54 lost five 'Dora-9s' in the combat, and No 486 Sqn lost a single Tempest and its pilot.

Two days later No 56 Sqn's Jim Payton was involved in another combat against superior Luftwaffe forces. After strafing a train, eight Tempests found themselves facing diving attacks from groups of Focke-Wulf and Messerschmitt fighters that were part of a formation of '50+' they had encountered. While fighting off these attacks in a confused melee, the Tempests lost two of their number, but claimed one destroyed, one probable and four damaged in return. Three of the latter category were later re-assessed as destroyed, two being credited to Flg Off Payton, setting him on the path to becoming No 56 Sqn's top-scorer.

On the same day (29 December) Typhoons were involved in air combat, having been 'bounced' while attacking ground targets. The units involved were Nos 168 and 439 Sqns, both of which were from No 143 Wing RCAF, the former operating as a 'fighter' unit and the

Few Tempests in 2nd TAF carried personal markings other than a discrete-applied wife or girlfriends' name. Tempest EJ705 'W2-X' of No 80 Sqn, however, was usually flown by Australian pilots within that unit, so it sported an appropriate badge depicting a kangaroo carrying an Australian flag. This Tempest destroyed three Bf 109s and a Fw 190 while being flown by four different pilots. Note the fresh 'Medium Sea Grey' paint on the underside where 'Invasion stripes' have been painted out (*IWM FLM 3115*)

latter in the fighter-bomber role. This meant that the Typhoons were able to fight back unencumbered by rocket rails. Honours were even, the Typhoons losing three of their number in exchange for claims of three destroyed. One of the Canadian pilots, Flg Off Bob Laurence of No 439 Sqn, was credited with two of them (a Bf 109 and a Fw 190).

After the mud, the Tempest air- and groundcrews had snow to cope with at Volkel. From early January 1945 all 2nd TAF aircraft had 'Invasion stripes' and their 'Sky' rear fuselage bands painted out. At the same time, spinners were painted black, and all roundels were modified to type 'C1' – red/white/blue, with a narrow yellow outer ring. The purpose of the changes was to distinguish the RAF aircraft from Luftwaffe fighters wearing 'Defence of the Reich' bands, and also to emphasise the RAF roundels to other Allied aircraft (*W J Hibbert*)

BODENPLATTE

On the first day of the New Year the Luftwaffe launched the ambitious assault Operation *Bodenplatte* on Allied airfields in Holland and Belgium, utilising every fighter it could muster – over 800. The operation met with mixed results, catching the defences by surprise, and finding many airfields full of targets, but in some cases failing to take advantage of their situation by carrying out poorly organised and delivered attacks.

The Allies had over 200 aircraft destroyed, and many more damaged, but few pilots were lost – the 2nd TAF had 12 killed and one made a PoW, but crucially, the Luftwaffe lost upwards of 200 pilots killed or taken prisoner and around 300 fighters. Allied losses could have been higher had the attack come a little earlier, for the German fighters arrived over the airfields some time after the early morning patrols had departed. This not only reduced the numbers of targets, but also meant that the returning Allied patrols were able to intervene. Several Tempest aces-to-be were involved in the action.

In the Paderborn-Bielefeld area No 486 Sqn were on an 'armed recce' when 'Kenway' reported Eindhoven under attack. Dropping tanks, Sqn Ldr 'Spike' Umbers led his eight Tempests back towards Allied territory at speed. In a series of combats, No 486 Sqn picked off six stragglers, Umbers claiming two (a Fw 190 and then a Bf 109). Plt Off Jimmy Sheddan also destroyed a Fw 190 for his first victory.

Meanwhile, No 56 Sqn were returning from Munster and heard No 486 Sqn's action over the R/T. Speeding towards their base, Flg Off Dave Ness eventually spotted a solitary Bf 109 pursued by two Tempests. When they broke off to return to base, Ness moved in, and with the help of Plt Off 'Artie' Shaw, caused the enemy fighter to crash land near Helmond. This was the latter pilot's fifth victory, making him the first Tempest ace, with two solo and three shared kills. At 32, he was much older than the average Tempest pilot, but had achieved this feat in just three weeks.

Volkel had been barely touched by the Luftwaffe attackers, and Sqn Ldr 'Spud' Spurdle was able to get nine No 80 Sqn Tempests airborne. 'Judy' Garland soon spotted a fighter low down and dived to

On 21 March 1945 Sqn Ldr Evan 'Rosie' Mackie led a formation of 16 No 80 Sqn Tempests on a sortie for the benefit of the RAF Film Unit. Mackie was flying his usual mount at that time, NV700 'W2-A' (*IWM FLM 3117*)

investigate, the aircraft proving to be 'long-nose' Fw 190. He also spied a second one some distance ahead. Garland overhauled both and despatched them in turn. Having destroyed another Fw 190 four days earlier, these were his third and fourth victories, leading to the award of a DFC and a posting to command a flight of No 3 Sqn. Sadly, he was shot down by flak on 8 February 1945 before he had chance to add to his score.

This view of a No 486 Sqn Tempest taxying at Volkel in mid-March 1945 clearly shows the modified roundels, correctly proportioned, above the wings. It was standard practice to have an 'erk' on the wing while taxying, as the view from the cockpit was poor, as was the condition of the taxyways. 'SA-X' was EJ888 at this time (*RNZAF*)

Typhoons were also among the 2nd TAF claimants on this action-packed day. No 439 Sqn's Bob Laurence was returning from a weather reconnaissance when he led four Typhoons in to attack a group of Fw 190s. Although he claimed two fighters destroyed, he was only allowed one destroyed and a probable. Had he been credited with both, he would have been the most successful Typhoon pilot in air combat between D-Day and VE-Day. As it was, he had to share that position with Johnny Baldwin and his No 2 that day, Flg Off Hugh Fraser, who destroyed two Fw 190s in the same combat (one of them a 'Dora'). Fraser would claim his third kill in February.

Replacement aircraft were ferried in from the UK to replace 2nd TAF's losses, and operations were soon at the pace established before the attack. On 4 January Dave Ness claimed his fifth victory. It all began, once again, following an attack on a train. Ness and Flt Lt J H Ryan had stayed at 6000 ft to cover the other four Tempests attacking the train when they saw two Bf 109s orbiting about a mile away. The Tempests attacked in a shallow dive, and as Ryan closed on the rear of his chosen target, the other Bf 109 climbed and Ness followed. The combat report suggests Ness's opponent was one of the many inexperienced pilots the Luftwaffe was now forced to commit to action;

'After a short dog-fight, and just as I was in position to fire from 100 yds, almost line astern, the hun broke away, did an aileron turn, and jettisoned his canopy. I followed him down about 2000 ft., & then up again,

Another shot of No 486 Sqn Tempests taken in March 1945. Note the temporary huts which served as accommodation for RAF personnel at Volkel (*RNZAF*)

noticing that by this time the pilot was half out of his cockpit. I fired a short burst from 150-50 yds., 10° to starboard, and saw strikes on the starboard wing. The pilot completed his baling out, and the a/c crashed and exploded in an open field. The pilot delayed pulling his ripcord to about 1000 ft. & the chute opened.'

The third pilot credited with five destroyed while flying Tempests, and the first to make five solo claims, was David 'Foob' Fairbanks who, on 14 January, made another double claim to reach this total. His

67

No 33 Sqn arrived too late in the campaign to produce any Tempest aces, but they did have their successes. Only four days after their arrival their CO, Sqn Ldr Matthew, along with South African Flt Lt L C Luckhoffa, shot down three Bf 109s. Two of these were credited to Luckhoff, who is seen here after the sortie in the cockpit of EJ880 '5R-R', which was hit by flak on the return journey (*IWM CL 2318*)

first victim was a Bf 109 which attempted to attack one of Fairbanks' formation. Rolling in behind the enemy, Fairbanks made short work of his opponent with a one-second burst. Five minutes later a single Fw 190 was seen following the railway line to Rheda. His combat report reveals one of the problems faced by Tempest pilots tackling Fw 190s at low level;

'I overhauled the Hun quite rapidly, and when I was about 800-600 yards he did a sharp break to Starboard. I couldn't hold him in this and passed about 100 yards behind. I throttled right back and continued turning. This went on for about a turn and a half and just as it looked as though I would be able to turn inside him he straightened out and started to climb up, turning slightly to Port. I was able to close nicely and fired a one-second burst from 200 yards and about 20° off.

'I didn't see strikes at first and decreased my deflection and fired a long burst. I observed lots of strikes on the mainplanes and fuselage, and the cockpit. A very large piece fell away from the E/A when I was approx 75 yards behind. I pulled up to avoid this and stalled and lost sight of him. I regained control just in time to see the E/A heading straight down from

Pilots of No 274 Sqn in March 1945. The CO, 'Jesse' Hibbert, is holding the squadron badge – he made four air combat claims while flying Tempests which, when added to his previous claims while flying Spitfires with Nos 124 and 126 Sqns, brought his score to four and two shared destroyed and two damaged. Another No 274 Sqn pilot with four confirmed destroyed in the air on Tempests was Flt Lt Pierre Clostermann, who can be seen standing third from the left in this photo (*W J Hibbert*)

about 1500 ft. He went in like that and blew up.'

On 23 January No 122 Wing had a day of air combat which would remain unequalled by the end of the war. All five squadrons of the Wing made claims, which after due assessments and revisions (as further evidence became available) eventually totalled 23 enemy aircraft destroyed. Among the claimants were No 486 Sqn's CO,

'Spike' Umbers, whose Bf 109 destroyed made him the next Tempest pilot to join the ranks of the aces, and one of only two to achieve their five kills on Typhoons and Tempests. Unfortunately, he would not enjoy this status for long, as he fell to flak while attacking barges on a canal just three weeks later. Jim Payton knocked down a Fw 190 for his fourth victory, 'Rosie' Mackie shot down a Bf 109 near Hesepe airfield for his second Tempest claim (and 19th overall) and 'Vass' Vassiliades added two Fw 190s destroyed and a third damaged to his score. The combats were virtually one-sided, and not a single Tempest was lost.

On 14 February Flg Off Hugh Fraser claimed his third victory (as mentioned earlier), thus showing that the Typhoon could also get the better of jets in the right circumstances. Four Typhoons of No 439 Sqn were reforming after attacking a train when two Me 262s (bomb-carrying aircraft of I./KG(J) 51) were sighted by Flt Lt Lyle Shaver and Fraser. The latter pilot later recalled the events in *Me 262 Combat Diary;*

'While we were looking for our own third and fourth aircraft we both spotted two Me 262s break through the cloud cover climbing in the same direction (west) as we were headed. Lyle reported them on the R/T at 2 o'clock almost directly below us and ordered the attack. We turned over and dove down on them at 60° angle or more. Halfway down they spotted us and broke down to port heading for the cloud cover about 1500 ft below them. At 400 yards Lyle was abreast of me, about 200 ft to starboard. The Me 262s were also about 200 ft apart, and the starboard aircraft was trailing the other one by 200 ft. We were doing over 500 mph and my aircraft was vibrating badly.

'I fired at the port aircraft and saw no hits. Lyle must have been firing on the other one which was now only 100 yards ahead of me and 200 ft to the right; we were closing on them very fast. I was firing again and at this moment Lyle's target exploded in a black cloud about 200 ft across. Later Lyle said he had flown through it and had picked up some pieces in his radiator. By now I was 100 yards from the other one, firing, and saw hits on the port engine and fuselage. My last burst was from 50 yards, and the port engine came off and went by just under me, as well as a section of wing. This had folded up from the engine nacelle outward, came off, and went under me flat not looking like much. I pulled up to avoid colliding with the Me 262. The moment I pulled up we were into cloud, and out the bottom of it a couple of seconds later, still in a 45° dive. I recovered and pulled up in a circle to 1500 ft, and saw the jet burst into flames as it hit the ground, without a ripple from any bomb it might have carried.'

With over 2000 hp of Sabre howling, a pair of No 274 Sqn Tempests lift off from the Sommerfeld tracking at Kluis (B.91) in April 1945. Note radiator flaps are open and both carry 45-gallon drop tanks – standard fit on 2nd TAF Tempests (*RAF Museum C E Brown 6049-1*)

Flt Lt Pierre Clostermann, author of the renowned *Le Grand Cirque* (*The Big Show*), joined No 274 Sqn in March 1945 after seeing extensive combat in Spitfires with Nos 341 and 602 Sqns. he enjoyed immediate success with the big Hawker fighter, downing a Bf 109 while undertaking a 'cannon test' (*R V Dennis*)

Former Typhoon pilot 'Hyphen' Taylor-Cannon had been promoted to command No 486 Sqn, and on 24 February he followed his predecessor in claiming a fifth confirmed victory – a Bf 109 shot down near Achmer airfield brought his final score to four and one shared destroyed and one probable.

Flying with No 56 Sqn as a supernumerary squadron leader at this time was Rhodesian Perry St Quintin. He had flown with No 33 Sqn in Egypt and had claimed a number of victories. His exact score is not known, as his log, and No 33 Sqn's records for this period, are missing, but he is credited in *Aces High* with at least seven confirmed during his time in Egypt. He was able to add two more while flying Tempests.

By coincidence, St Quintin's old squadron, No 33, was one of two which had traded their Spitfires for Tempests and rejoined 2nd TAF early. The other new Tempest unit was No 222 Sqn, and both outfits joined No 135 Wing at Gilze-Rijen. The other Tempest Wing had a change of leader at this time, as John Wray's tour had come to an end. He was relieved by Peter Brooker, who had commanded No 123 Wing during the Normandy campaign.

On 4 March another ace – perhaps the best known Tempest exponent of them all – entered the fray. Free French pilot Pierre Clostermann had already completed a lengthy tour of operations with Nos 341 and 602 Sqns, and at this time was credited with seven destroyed, two probable and seven damaged. After a hair-raising conversion to Typhoons at Aston Down (as described in his gripping and atmospheric book, *Le Grand Cirque*, published in English as *The Big Show*), he arrived at Volkel and joined No 274 Sqn as a supernumerary flight lieutenant.

Clostermann opened his score on Tempests on only his second day at Volkel while carrying out a 'cannon test' on Tempest EJ893 'JJ-W' – these occasions were often used as an excuse for free ranging sorties. He came across a section of Typhoons closely followed by four Bf 109s in line abreast, apparently intent on making an attack. Wasting no time, the Frenchman dived on the Messerschmitts, latching on to one when the formation broke. After firing three bursts, he was forced to retreat into cloud cover as the other Bf 109s had come to their comrade's aid, but after orbiting on instruments for a short while, he finally broke cloud to find his target burning on the ground.

The next pilot to join the ranks of Tempest aces was No 56 Sqn's Jim Payton who, on 7 March, brought down a Fw 190 with two short bursts in that fruitful hunting ground for Tempests, the Rheine area.

Sqn Ldr 'Jesse' Hibbert's usual aircraft when commanding No 274 Sqn in March 1945 was NV722 'JJ-M'. Pierre Clostermann also flew this Tempest on at least two operational sorties (*W J Hibbert*)

Flt Lt Pierre Clostermann in Tempest NV994 'JF-E', photographed by Charles E Brown from an Auster in the closing weeks of the war (*RAF Museum/Charles E Brown*)

FINAL BATTLES

After a lengthy period of stalemate on the ground, the Allies launched their massive operation to cross the Rhine on 24 March 1945. For the next six weeks an ever more desperate Luftwaffe would be brought to battle with increasing frequency. April proved to be the most productive, in terms of air combat victories, for the Tempest squadrons, with 62 enemy aircraft claimed destroyed in the air during the month, and a further 22 in the first three days of May. Hostilities ceased on 4 May 1945.

During this period, Ness, Payton, Clostermann and Mackie all added to their scores, but the highest scorer was a newcomer. Flt Lt Warren 'Smokey' Schrader had flown Spitfires with No 1435 Sqn in Malta and Sicily, destroying two Bf 109Gs and sharing a third. Now, having completed a tour as an instructor, the New Zealander joined No 486 Sqn, and in just 12 days scored five victories. By the cessation of hostilities he had claimed nine and one shared destroyed on Tempests (second only to Fairbanks), risen to command No 486 Sqn, and been further promoted to Wing Commander in charge of the first Meteor jet unit, No 616 Sqn!

Schrader's run of success began on 10 April when he pounced on a Fw 190 which was positioning to attack a formation of Typhoons. Three days later Sqn Ldr Taylor-Cannon, who had assumed command of No 486 Sqn when Umbers was lost, himself fell victim to flak. A direct hit from an '88' while attacking 'MET' (mechanised enemy transport) forced a low-level bale out, and no trace was ever found of the popular 'Hyphen', despite extensive postwar enquiries.

It would be a week before Schrader was confirmed as the new CO, and in that time he made three more claims – two Fw 190s on 15 April and another the following day. The combat on 15 April had seen nine Tempests engage nine Fw 190s, with the New Zealanders claiming eight of their counterparts destroyed and one damaged for the loss off one of their number (who baled out and managed to reach Allied lines). Appointed CO on 21 April, Schrader claimed his fifth Tempest kill on the same day. Five kills had come in just 12 days, but it would be a further eight days before he made the next additions to his score. The delay was compensated for by a claim of three and one shared destroyed! The combat report highlights the accurate shooting that makes an ace, which was all the more impressive as Tempests were fitted with the standard reflector sight, not the gyro gun sight which some Spitfires boasted by this time;

'After manoeuvring, I fired a shoot burst from 300 yards with 30° angle off. I saw strikes on the Port side of the engine and at the lower part of the cockpit. The Fw 190 went into a slow steep spiral and

Tempest top scorer in the last four weeks of hostilities was 'Smokey' Schrader of No 486 Sqn with nine and one shared destroyed. He rose from flight lieutenant to wing commander in the same period, leading No 616 Sqn for the last few days of the war – the only Allied jet unit to see action (*via P Sortehaug*)

Schrader's aircraft during this period was NV969 'SA-A', which he used to destroy four Fw 190s and three and one shared Bf 109s (*via P Sortehaug*)

When Schrader was promoted to wing commander, his place as CO of No 486 Sqn was taken by Jimmy Sheddan, who made his last three claims while flying SN129 'SA-M' (*C J Sheddan*)

I saw it crash and explode on the ground.

'Shortly after this engagement I saw a M.E.109 with 1 bomb centre-slung flying 12 o'clock towards us. The E/A broke Port and within 300 yards I fired a burst with 60° angle off. I saw strikes on the Port wing root followed by a vivid flash. The E/A rolled on its back and went straight into the deck.'

Ten minutes later another Bf 109 was sighted and attacked, first by his No 2 and then by Schrader himself. This was a relatively simple target, with the Tempests closing in from 'dead line astern' and the enemy aircraft rolling over streaming white smoke, before crashing into the ground and exploding. Shortly after this, two more Bf 109s were seen heading towards Hamburg;

'We chased them to the area of Hamburg airport. I attacked the leader instructing my No.2 to attack the other. After a short dogfight I fired a 2 second burst from 300 yards with 20° angle off and saw strikes on the Port side of the engine. The 109 caught fire immediately and dived in flames steeply to the deck where it crashed on the secondary railway line just S.E. of the Hamburg A/D.'.

Despite the rest of No 486 Sqn having lost contact with their leader after the first combat, they had also seen action – total claims were six destroyed, one probable and two damaged for no loss to the Tempests.

Another pilot who made startling advances in April 1945 was Jimmy Sheddan, one of No 486 Sqn's New Zealanders who had started his tour on Typhoons back in May 1943, and flown continuously on operations but for two short breaks owing to injury. Promoted to command the flight previously led by Schrader, he again stepped into his former CO's shoes on 2 May to take command of No 486 Sqn.

At the same time Sheddan's score mounted, with two Ju 87s on 6 April, a Fw 190 on 14 April, a share in another two days later and finally a 'four-engined flying boat' shared destroyed. The Ju 87s were an unusual target for Tempests at this stage of the war, and were probably from one of the *Nachtschlachtgruppen* (night ground attack groups) units.

Jimmy Sheddan is seen seated in SN129 soon after taking command of No 486 Sqn (*C J Sheddan*)

On 12 April Jack Stafford – by now 'A' Flight commander of No 486 Sqn – claimed his fifth kill while flying Sheddan's Tempest (SN129 'SA-M'), beating the latter to ace status by two days. On the same day, No 56 Sqn's Flg Off Dave Ness claimed a Fw 190 for his final victory, and six days earlier Flg Off Jim Payton had also destroyed a Fw 190. With five and one shared destroyed and six destroyed respectively, these were the unit's top scorers.

Although, generally speaking, losses were relatively low among the Tempest squadrons, with flak the pre-eminent cause, some aircraft were also shot down by the few remaining German fighters encountered, with none more painful a loss being that of Wg Cdr Peter Brooker. On 16 April Brooker led a section of No 80 Sqn north-west of Berlin and attacked a train near Neuruppin. It seems that his aircraft was hit and caught fire, and whilst struggling with the hood release, the Wing Leader and his No 2 were 'bounced' by Fw 190s and shot down.

The area where both men crashed became Russian territory after the war, and confirmation of the fate and resting place of this veteran of the Battle of Britain, Far East and Normandy, who had perished just three weeks before the ceasefire, was never forthcoming. Like thousands of his comrades with no known graves, he is commemorated on the Runneymede memorial.

After a two-week delay, Brooker's place was taken by Evan Mackie, who had added to his score twice during April. On the 9th No 80 Sqn had caught a number of aircraft in the circuit at Fassberg, and Mackie's share was two 'Me108s' destroyed, although stills from his combat film show that the aircraft were in fact Arado Ar 96 trainers. These were his fourth and fifth confirmed kills while flying Tempests, and he made his final air combat claim six days later – a Fw 190 shared with Sgt Turner (missing with Brooker the next day).

After missing the last half of April by taking No 80 Sqn to the Armament Practice Camp at Warmwell, back in the UK, Mackie returned to Germany as Wing Commander Flying No 122 Wing, but only had the opportunity to add aircraft destroyed on the ground to his total. His final score, the highest of any pilot to fly Tempests on operations, was 20 and 3 shared destroyed, 2 probably destroyed, 8 and 1 shared damaged, 3 and 1 shared destroyed on the ground and 1 damaged on the ground.

This latter statement may well be controversial in view of the total of victories frequently attributed to Pierre Clostermann. We last mentioned him claiming his first Tempest kill with No 274 Sqn on 5 March, but by the middle of that month he had been posted to No 56 Sqn as a flight commander. With this unit he destroyed a Fi 156 on the ground on 28 March, followed by a Fw 190 destroyed in the air and two Ju 188s damaged on the ground on 2 April, and two Fw 190Ds damaged in the air on 5 April. Three days later Clostermann transferred to No 3 Sqn as 'A' Flight commander, making a single air combat claim with this unit – two Fw 190s destroyed on 20 April (believed to be 'Dora 9s' of II./JG 26).

On an early morning patrol on 3 May, he destroyed one Fw 190 and damaged two more all on the ground at a strip five miles east of Oldenburg. Later in the day, in an attack on Grossenbrode land and seaplane base, he claimed one Do 24 destroyed and six other aircraft

When Wg Cdr Peter Brooker was posted missing in action, the position of Wing Commander Flying No 122 Wing was filled by Evan Mackie, who is seen here in front of his appropriately marked Tempest, SN228. He did not take up the post until 2 May 1945, when he chose the newly-delivered SN228 as his personal mount (*E D Mackie*)

SN228 is seen in close-up with a Buckeburg groundcrew member in the cockpit. The scoreboard was almost certainly added after the war. Note the single Italian marking among the swastikas (*R Abrahams via H Smallwood*)

This overall view of SN228 also reveals a unit crest on the aircraft's tail which, like the scoreboard, was probably a postwar addition (*Chris Shores*)

Typhoon ace 'Pinkie' Stark returned from rest to command his old unit, No 609 Sqn, for the last two months of the war. He flew SW411 'PR-J', marked with his squadron leader's pennant and (just visible to the right of it) No 609's white rose and hunting horns, which had first adorned their Typhoons three years earlier (*L W F Stark*)

Flt Lt Jim Payton steadily accumulated victories throughout his tour with No 56 Sqn, finishing the war as its top scorer (six destroyed) in Typhoons, a position he shared with Flg Off David Ness (five and 1 shared destroyed). He was shot down by small arms fire on 24 April 1945, but survived as a PoW (*J J Payton*)

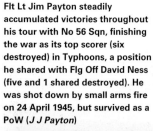

damaged, these being all on land or water. After assessment, he was in fact credited with two Do 24s and a Ju 352 destroyed, plus two Bv 138s and two Ar 232s damaged. Finally, on 4 May he destroyed two Do 18s on the water at Schleswig seaplane base.

This list totals four destroyed and two damaged in the air, and six destroyed and six damaged on the ground (or sea), bringing the Frenchman's final score (including Spitfire claims) to 11 destroyed, 2 probables and 9 damaged in the air and 6 destroyed and 6 damaged on the ground.

The controversy arises when this total is compared with the scoreboard painted on Clostermann's postwar Tempest NV724 'JF-E', which showed 23 black and white German crosses plus a further 9 white outlines. In addition, Clostermann has a list of victories, totalling 19 and 14 shared destroyed, 5 probables and 7 damaged, plus a further 4 destroyed on the ground, 3 probables and 13 damaged, compiled in November 1945 and signed by Air Vice Marshal Harry Broadhurst.

It must be pointed out, however, that the sources used in calculating Clostermann's score for this publication are the same as those used for all the other pilots mentioned, namely the Squadron Operations Record Books (Forms 540 and 541), Combat Reports and, most importantly, the 2nd TAF Log of Casualty Claims, Assessments and Losses (and a similar Fighter Command document for earlier claims). This latter document recorded all combat claims, the results of their assessment and any subsequent amendment, and has been taken as the ultimate arbiter in the case of disputed claims. These sources were also the key references used by the authors of *Aces High* (the most detailed and comprehensive survey of RAF aces), against which the findings for this work were checked.

TOP SCORERS

The two top scoring pilots on Typhoons and Tempests, Johnny Baldwin and David Fairbanks, make interesting comparisons. Baldwin, an Englishman, had a meteoric rise, going from pilot officer to group captain in just over two years. When his flying training was complete he went straight to an operational squadron, with only 350 hours flying experience. He accumulated 16 enemy aircraft confirmed destroyed in the course of two operational tours.

Fairbanks, a US citizen who had joined the RCAF, reached the rank of squadron leader in about the same period. He had spent a prolonged spell as a flight instructor before reaching an operational unit, and went on to score all but one of his twelve victories in less than two-and-a-half months. Both had an additional kill that could be added to their scores.

Grp Capt J R Baldwin DSO, DFC

Born in Bath four months before the end of World War 1, John Robert Baldwin joined the RAFVR as soon as World War 2 started. Following service as groundcrew in the Battle of France, and on bomb disposal duties during the Blitz, he was selected for aircrew training and was one of the first trainees to take advantage of the Arnold Scheme (in which RAF pilots were trained to 'wings' standard at USAAF training schools).

On returning to the UK, following advanced and operational training at No 59 OTU, Baldwin was posted to No 609 Sqn, at Manston, on 18 November 1942. His potential must have been obvious to justify his posting direct from a training unit to a Typhoon squadron at the forefront of operations, and whoever made the decision had ample cause to reflect on the accuracy of their judgement.

Baldwin's first flight in the Typhoon took place on 22 November, and by the middle of the following month he had accumulated less than ten hours on type. On the afternoon of 15 December he took off from Manston for 'air firing practice' at the Goodwin Sands, in the English Channel. While firing at the sandbanks, he heard over the R/T that Red Section of No 609 Sqn were attempting to intercept intruders. Orbiting the Goodwins, he soon spotted a Fw 190 diving for

Plt Off J R Baldwin with R7713 'PR-Z', his most regular aircraft from November 1942 to February 1943 (*J R Baldwin*)

75

This Fw 190 was shot down by Baldwin on 28 August 1943 while flying Typhoon JP583 'PR-A' on a 'Ranger' to the south-west of Paris (*J R Baldwin*)

Looking every inch the ace, and squadron commander, Baldwin is seen seated in the cockpit of 'TP-Z', with its scoreboard showing 13$\frac{1}{2}$ victories, although his official score was 12$\frac{1}{2}$ at the time. See the text for an explanation of this anomaly and the profile commentaries for the probable identity of this aircraft (*via D Sweeting*)

the Belgian coast.

Despite opening to full throttle, he was unable to close on the Focke-Wulf 1000 yards ahead, but a long range burst caused the German pilot to weave, and he was able to gain a little. Firing short bursts, he eventually saw strikes with sparks and smoke from the engine. He was now able to close to within 300 yards but, poised for the kill, he now found he was out of ammunition. Not only that, but a Bf 109 had appeared uncomfortably close behind him. He was able to make a rapid turn for base, however, while the Luftwaffe aircraft continued towards the French coast. 'Air firing practice' had become the real thing, and the novice operational pilot had opened his score with the claim of 'one Fw 190 damaged'.

The next five weeks were occupied by fruitless 'anti-Rhubarb' patrols between North Foreland and Dungeness. However, on 20 January 1943 Baldwin was on standby at Manston when he received the order to 'scramble'. The Luftwaffe had launched a fighter-bomber operation against London, and the first wave of 34 Fw 190s (which had prompted the scramble) escaped with only one loss. The second wave, consisting of Fw 190s and Bf 109G fighter-bombers, were not so lucky. With Flg Off Creteur for company, Baldwin received instructions to climb to the east of Manston, eventually sighting eight Bf 109s (of 6./JG 26) at 20,000 ft. The Typhoon was out of its element at this height, but Baldwin did not hesitate, attacking immediately. His combat report read as follows;

'The formation broke up and I fired at aircraft that came close and on which I could see black crosses. I saw three of these break away from the melee and so followed these which preceded south towards Dover. I closed with one on the left and fired a burst at 100 yards or less, getting thick black smoke so immediately turned on the next and fired at that also from 100 yards or less dead astern. This aeroplane disintegrated completely, pieces flying all over the sky, and as it exploded the starboard wing of the first plane I fired at fell off as he went into a slight diving turn. The aeroplane went spinning towards the sea.

'By this time the 3rd 109 was on my tail but shutting the throttle and skidding with full rudder in a climbing turn he passed me and as I was about to fire half rolled and dived. I followed catching him up rapidly and again at about 100 yards I fired seeing strikes on the underside of his plane, but overshot him before I could get in a long burst. I pulled away to one side again and saw him continuing the dive but turning toward Dover where there was a layer of cloud into which he went. There I lost him, and could not see him above or below cloud, but soon saw a parachute at about 8,000 ft. I circled this, informing control and giving a long call on button D. I saw him hit the water and float for some minutes and then he appeared to sink so I returned home. On landing I found one tyre and the main petrol tank had been punctured by a bullet.'

Ten days later Baldwin helped to interview two of his victims, one of whom had spent two days in his dinghy. They expressed surprise at having been vanquished by 'a worm' like Baldwin, and believed they had been attacked by a 'Vultee Vanguard' or a 'Mustang'! His superiors, however, were more impressed, and Baldwin's unhesitating and effective action brought him his first DFC.

The routine of patrols, interspersed by occasional 'Rhubarbs', continued until 25 March, when Baldwin discovered what it was like to be on the receiving end. 'Bounced' by two Fw 190s from 5./JG 26 following a 'scramble', he was shot down off Ramsgate, managing to bale out from his burning and spinning aircraft at 1000 ft. With burnt hands, and unable to deploy his dinghy, he was fortunate to be picked up by an air-sea rescue launch after just 35 minutes.

He returned to duty after three weeks in hospital and three weeks of sick leave to find that 'intruders' were now the order of the day. Even so, it was August before he had a chance to engage the Luftwaffe in combat again. With enemy aircraft rarely seen on the Channel coast, Baldwin, now a flight commander, and his CO, Sqn Ldr Pat Thornton-Brown, were determined to seek out the opposition. On the 28th of the month, after strenuous efforts to obtain two pairs of long-range tanks, which were not yet in general use, they undertook a long-range 'Rhubarb' to the south of Paris, where each pilot despatched a Fw 190. This was the victory which took Baldwin to the magic 'five down', making him the first pilot to achieve this feat solely while flying Typhoons. Having established the feasibility of such operations, known as 'Rangers', No 609 Sqn would lead the way in developing the art over the coming months.

Meanwhile the patrols and 'Rhubarbs' continued, but now with increasing escort missions, sometimes to Typhoon bombers, or to anti-shipping Beaufighters or medium bombers. It was, however, on another 'Ranger' on 4 October that Baldwin next added to his mounting score. With Belgian Sgt Henrion as his No 2, various ground targets were attacked before sighting two Bf 109Gs. The Typhoons turned sharply to make a stern attack on the enemy aircraft, Baldwin firing bursts at both, which produced strikes and smoke in both cases and stopped the engine of the second target. Henrion also hit the second Bf 109, and both pilots were each subsequently credited with a Bf 109 destroyed apiece.

The Belgian's 'kill' seems to have been a generous gesture on the flight commander's part, for Baldwin remarked in his log '1 given to No 2'. It also perhaps explains why Baldwin's Typhoon, in March 1944, was marked with $13\frac{1}{2}$ kills when his official score was only $12\frac{1}{2}$. The 'half' followed later in the month, on 16 October, when Baldwin shared a Ju 88 with Pat Thornton-Brown on a 'Ranger' to Bretigny, near Paris.

At the end of November 1943, the CO of No 198 Sqn (No 609's sister-Typhoon unit at Manston) was due to go on 'rest', and Johnny Baldwin was selected as his replacement. 'Sprog' Typhoon pilot to Typhoon squadron CO in a year! On his first operation with his new command (although led by the retiring CO), he was forced to turn back with engine trouble – to Baldwin's frustration, the formation went on to claim five kills over Holland (see Chapter Three).

The very next day he made up for the missed action on a 'Fortress Support Sweep' over Luftwaffe bases in Holland, when three Fw 190s

With a backdrop of wrecked terminal buildings at Deurne (B.70), Antwerp's pre-war civil airfield, groundcrew are busy with PD521 'JB II', which was one of Wg Cdr Baldwin's Typhoons. Soon after joining No 146 Wing he had adopted two Hawker fighters as his personal aircraft and had them marked 'JB I' and 'JB II' – one was armed with bombs and the other rockets. PD521 was his third 'JB II', the numeral 'II' in this photo being obscured by a fitter's arm (*RAF Museum - Charles E Brown 299-33A*)

were surprised in the circuit at Marskamp, and one fell to Baldwin's guns. Three days later and another 'Ranger', this time to Eindhoven, where carnage was visited upon the Do 217s of KG 2 (see Chapter Three) – one was credited to Baldwin, taking his score to eight and one shared. Three more sweeps in December failed to encounter the Luftwaffe, and the rest of the month was mainly spent escorting obsolescent Hurricane IVs on their last sorties before these units were themselves equipped with Typhoons.

In the New Year the pace of the action stepped up again, beginning with an attack on 1 January 1944 on the *Munsterland*, which was heavily defended by flak in Boulogne harbour. Baldwin was first in to the attack, silencing the ship's own guns, followed by eight more Typhoons – two fitted with rockets – which caused an explosion amidships. Five of No 198 Sqn's Typhoons were hit by ferocious flak from the shore and surrounding flak ships, but all returned to Manston, although two made crash landings. The next day another productive 'Ranger' was flown, Baldwin stalking and destroying a Fw 190 intent on landing, while other pilots found their skills challenged by 'dogfights' with Bu 131 trainers, which proved difficult targets – only one was destroyed and one damaged.

After a couple of 'Rangers' were aborted due to bad weather, success came again on 13 January when Baldwin led six Typhoons to sweep around Luftwaffe bases north and north-east of Paris. Four of the six pilots involved were, or would be, aces – Baldwin, Bryan (making a 'guest' appearance whilst on 'rest'), Niblett and Eagle. Between them, four enemy aircraft were destroyed in the air – two Goeland transports and two Bf 109s. Baldwin's share was one of the transports, which he stalked in similar fashion to the Fw 190 12 days earlier.

A separate operation on the same day also netted four kills for No 198 Sqn (three Ju 88s and an Ar 96), Baldwin's aggressive leadership proving most effective yet again. More mundane duties – escorts to Beaufighters, Mosquitoes or Hurricanes – occupied the rest of January until the 30th, when the two Manston units, Nos 198 and 609, set out to cover Luftwaffe bases in the Paris area prior to a raid by 200 USAAF Marauders.

At last the Luftwaffe seemed to be responding the threat posed by the Typhoons over recent weeks, for the formation was intercepted by Fw 190s. First came six in line abreast, at tree-top height, followed by a second wave of '12+'. The Typhoons turned into the threat, both sides opening fire as they converged head-on. One Fw 190 went down almost immediately, and then the formation locked into a tight-turning, low-level, dogfight. Baldwin turned tightly behind one of the attackers, but broke off to destroy a Fw 190 latched on to the tail of Blue 1 (Flt Lt Dall).

After downing a second Fw 190, he climbed for cloud so as to evade three more fighters. On the way up he got a bird's eye view of the battle and, observing that the enemy had been steadily reinforcing until they numbered 40+, he gave the order to 'get into cloud and withdraw'.

This, incredibly, the Typhoon pilots managed to achieve without loss, the only damage suffered being a hit by light flak on Blue 2 during withdrawal. Back at base, the claims were totted up and No 198 Sqn's share was nine destroyed, one probable and two damaged – No 609 added another three destroyed. Their opponents were JG 2, who lost at least six Fw 190s.

In February Baldwin attended No 1 course of the newly-formed Fighter Leader School at Milfield, returning to No 198 Sqn briefly before the end of his tour in March. He had already been awarded a bar to his DFC for his work with No 198 Sqn, and this was now followed by the award of a DSO, and a spell on 'rest' as Squadron Leader (Tactics), 2 Group, 2nd TAF.

The D-Day invasion was just ten days old when the loss of Wg Cdr Baker brought Baldwin back to operations, and promotion as Wing Commander Flying, No 146 Wing. Posted on 19 June, he was in action the next day, leading No 257 Sqn in a bombing operation to seal the mouth of a railway tunnel. This was the first of at least 110 operational sorties flown by Baldwin in under four months – 'at least' because that is the total recorded in his logbook. However, No 146 Wing's official history states '170 ops since D-Day', and one of the squadron ORBs says '150+'. It would have been typical of the man to under-record his sorties flown in an effort to stay on operations longer.

During this period two more opportunities to add to his score presented themselves. The first was on 29 June, when Baldwin and nine Typhoons of No 193 Sqn ran into ragged formations of Bf 109s near Conches; the second, two weeks later, on 13 July, when he was leading three pilots of No 197 Sqn and met up with '15+' Bf 109Gs.

In both combats, Baldwin employed tactics he had developed during his 'Ranger' days – tight turns, accurate deflection shooting, good use of cloud cover and timely withdrawal when low on ammunition, or odds threatened to overwhelm. On the first occasion the Typhoon pilots were able to claim five destroyed and five damaged with no loss to themselves, two of the kills being credited to Baldwin. On the second, the four Typhoons were heavily outnumbered by the Bf

When Baldwin returned to operations as a group captain in charge of No 123 Wing, he again had two personal Typhoons bomb and rocket-equipped. Both were identically marked 'JB', and carried the serials SW496 and SW470. This close up shows Grp Capt Baldwin seated in the cockpit the latter fighter. Between him and the anonymous groundcrewman is his scoreboard, numbering 16 kills, and an appropriate rank pennant (*J R Baldwin*)

Both of Grp Capt Baldwin's 'JBs' are seen together probably at Plantlunne (B.103) in April or May 1945. Just visible above the wheels, on the inside of the undercarriage doors on both aircraft, is the 'JB' monogram, similar to the one worn on his Mae-West (*J R Baldwin*)

109s of JG 5, but Baldwin was able to shoot one down in reply to the loss of one Typhoon (which collided with a Messerschmitt, the pilot baling out to captivity) and a second heavily damaged. It was the last chance that Baldwin would have to bring his guns to bear on the Luftwaffe in the air, and his final score was 15 and 1 shared destroyed and 4 damaged.

In November 1944 Baldwin went 'on rest' again, this time as Wing Commander Planning at 84 Group Control Centre, but in February 1945 he managed to return to action, promoted again (to group captain) and with a bar to his DSO, as Officer Commanding No 123 Wing, which by happy chance numbered two of his old squadrons, Nos 198 and 609, among its four resident Typhoon units.

As a group captain, Baldwin was expected not to fly on 'ops', but he undertook at least another 16 before the war ended. Based at Wunstorf with his Wing for the rest of the year, he opted to remain in the RAF post-war and was sent to command the Fighter Test Squadron at Boscombe Down in 1946. Detachment to the Egyptian Air Force followed in 1948, and then command of No 249 Sqn (he was a squadron leader by now, having shed temporary wartime promotions like many of his comrades) in Iraq, flying Tempests. By early 1952 he was a wing commander once again, attached to the USAF's 16th Fighter Interceptor Squadron of the 51st Fighter Interceptor Wing, flying F-86 Sabres in Korea.

On 15 March 1952, after flying eight sorties on Sabres, he was reported missing from a weather reconnaissance in the Sariwon area. It seems that Baldwin's Sabre was not seen again after an attempted cloud break in mountainous country, although there have been unsubstantiated rumours that he was accidentally shot down by his wingman. There were also hopes that he had survived, stemming from reported sightings in Korean PoW camps, but extensive enquiries at the time, and recent attempts involving US and Russian sources, have been to no avail. The most successful Typhoon fighter pilot, and youthful leader of elite Typhoon Wings, remains 'missing in action'.

─────── Sqn Ldr D C Fairbanks DFC ───────

The son of a Cornell University professor, David Charles Fairbanks was some four years younger than Baldwin. He lived and breathed aviation from an early age, and in his final years at high school, he avidly followed the progress of the European air war. When his education was complete, he ran away from home, heading for Canada to join the RCAF. This enterprise having initially failed due to a lack of funds, he tried again in February 1941, and this time he managed to enlist at Hamilton.

On completion of his flying training Fairbanks was posted to the No 13 SFTS as an instructor. His ambitions to be involved in the air war frustrated, and he endured this role for a year. At last a posting to the UK came his way, and after advanced and operational training, he joined No 501 Sqn at Hawkinge, where he flew Spitfire Vs. It was with this unit that Fairbanks achieved his first combat victory, on D-Day plus two, when he destroyed a Bf 109 and damaged another near Le Havre.

With Tempest re-equipment in prospect for No 501 Sqn, a number of pilots, including Fairbanks, were posted to No 274 Sqn. This was fortunate for the budding ace as No 501 Sqn would specialise in the anti-'Diver' operations and remain in the UK, while No 274 Sqn would also re-equip with Tempests and then proceed to the Continent to join No 122 Wing. Before this move occurred, however, the unit performed anti-'Diver' sorties as well, with Fairbanks destroying two robot bombs.

Few enemy aircraft were encountered during No 274 Sqn's first weeks at Volkel, but many ground targets were sought out and attacked. On one of these sorties, on 19 November 1944, Fairbanks' Tempest received a hit in the leading edge of the port wing, setting the fuel tank on fire. Flames streamed from the ruptured wing, stripping the tail surfaces of paint and the rudder of fabric. Despite the damage he was able to return to Volkel and land safely, this exploit resulting in the awarding off a DFC.

The chance he'd been waiting for came at last on 17 December;

'I was flying Blue 1 on a sweep to Rheine and we had turned on to 270° at 2000 ft (I was slightly ahead of the C.O. and was weaving a little to slow down) and near Burgsteinfurt when I saw an A/c about 1000 ft below heading East. It passed under our formation and I immediately rolled on my back and gave chase. As I pulled out of the dive I recognised the E/a as a Me.109 and began to close in. The E/a pulled straight up and when I was about 500 yards behind it, it was in a stalled position standing on its tail. The pilot baled out, the aircraft bunted and went straight into the deck and I saw the Pilot land a short distance away in some trees.'

After shooting down a second Bf 109 from a formation of three, Fairbanks encountered two more;

'One was being chased by another Tempest and I broke onto the second one. This E/a continued straight and level just at the base of cloud (4000 ft). I quickly closed the range from below to approx 150 yards and fired but only my port cannons worked. After a few bursts I saw strikes on the E/a's starboard wing, he did only a very slight turn to starboard and continued on. I rolled on to him again and fired until my ammo ran out. I overhauled the E/a and came right under his wing for a few seconds – the pilot was looking out the opposite side and did not seem to have a clue! He finally saw me and I pulled over the top of him, gave the finger sign and came home.'

It has been stated that the damaged Bf 109 (the one to whose pilot Fairbanks made his gesture) was subsequently hit by Allied anti-aircraft fire, the pilot baling out and Fairbanks sharing the credit with the gunners. No mention of this has, however, been found in 2nd TAF records.

A posting to No 3 Sqn, also of No 122 Wing, came at the end of December, and the New Year saw Fairbanks' run of success continue throughout January with claims for a Fw 190 on 4 January, and another, along with a Bf 109, on 14 January, and a share in a Ju 52 on the 23rd.

On 9 February 1945 Fairbanks was posted back to No 274 Sqn to replace Sqn Ldr Baird, who had been posted missing the previous day (he had been shot down and killed by Bf 109s of JG 27). '"Foob" Fairbanks, the "terror of Rheine" is to return to us', enthused the Squadron diarist! Fairbanks was now able to exercise his talents to the full, claiming six more kills, and it would seem a seventh, in the next three weeks.

His first claim as CO came just two days after taking command. Leading his unit near Achmer, he led a section down to attack a train, and on rejoining the rest of the formation, he sighted, and gave chase to, a fast moving enemy aircraft which he later identified as a Me 262. The jet stayed above a cloud bank for a while and then dived out of sight.

One of No 274 Sqn's new Tempests, looking extremely business-like. It is believed to be EJ640 'JJ-G', which was flown on two of the unit's early Tempest operations by Flt Lt Fairbanks (*CAF*)

With damage reminiscent of that caused by V1 explosions, this is in fact Fairbanks' Tempest EJ627 'JJ-F' which was hit by flak on 19 November 1944. As well as the obvious damage to the tail unit, twisted metal on the leading edge marks the site where the cannon shell hit, setting the fuel tank on fire. Note also the missing panel above the ammunition bay, which must have added to Fairbanks' problems in controlling the aircraft. This episode played a major role in the award of his first DFC (*via A E Gunn*)

Fairbanks saw a small gap and took his chance to follow. Dropping out of cloud at about 2000 ft, he observed the aircraft also emerging about 1500 yards ahead and to port;

'He started a gentle turn to Starboard, saw us, and opened up, doing an orbit to Port. I followed 1500 yards behind and 1000 ft below. We continued on a straight course and I followed while going through small low patches of cloud and losing sight of him from time to time. We carried on for about 15/20 miles and evidently he thought he had lost us.

'As I came through a small patch of cloud I saw the E/A about 800 yards dead ahead at approx 1500 ft over Rheine A/Fd. He was just dropping his nose wheel and started to turn into Starboard. I dropped my tanks on seeing the airfield and closed to approx 250-300 yards and placed the bead on his starboard turbo and slightly above, firing a 1/2 second burst to test my deflection and saw little puffs of smoke on the fuselage and then a great burst of flame. The E/A went straight down immediately and blew up in the centre of Rheine A/Fd. My No.3 who was just behind me saw the E/A go down and blow up on one of the runways.'

Luftwaffe records show that the 'Me 262' was in fact one of the equally elusive Ar 234B jet reconnaissance bombers operated by 1(F)./123, and that this was the first one to be destroyed in the air by the Allied air forces. Three days later Fairbanks claimed another Me 262, but only as damaged, having had to break of his attack due the appearance of two more jet fighters, a shortage of ammunition and fierce flak from Plantlunne airfield. This latter hazard was always now evident in the region of German airfields, as Allied pilots tried to take advantage of returning Luftwaffe fighters – particularly the jets – at their most vulnerable time. On 16 February airfield flak again frustrated Fairbanks, when he had the chance of a triple claim. Sighting four Bf 109s, he gave the order to drop tanks and dived after three of them, their leader having stayed high;

'I followed them down and spent about 1 1/2 to 2 minutes trying to get

on to the end man. They were at about 500 ft. & I stayed about 1000 ft above taking an occasional pass at the No. 3 (without firing). The E/A seemed to have quite a few clues & every now and then they would pull up & fire at me, sometimes head-on. I kept it in a good position and called for the rest of Red section to come down. Finally the last man broke to pick up speed & I bounced him & managed to get a burst in from about 200 yds. and 20° off, and hit him in the rad. & in the fuselage. I broke as the other two started in behind me. I saw him again trying to make a forced landing & made a fast attack from dead astern & about 50 ft. off the deck. I last saw him belly in and break up on the ground.

'The other two started doing circles again & I dived at the end man & throttled back & fired from about 200 closing to 150 yds. & saw strikes on the rad. & some of my tracer hit the fuselage & he started to smoke. I broke as I overshot & just turned around in time to see him go straight in and blow up near the A/F at Hildesheim.

'I started after the 3rd & as I came up over a few houses I saw the A/F dead ahead & broke off the chase because of flak from the "drome".'

Fairbanks returned to this area (his favourite hunting ground) with further success on 22 February. Heading south from Plantlunne, he passed over Rheine airfield on an easterly heading and eight or ten Fw 190s were encountered – they were Fw 190Ds, known to pilots as 'Dora 9s'. Fairbanks picked out one to pursue in his usual aggressive manner, causing it to crash into the ground, apparently through its pilot's strenuous efforts to evade. Attacked by four more, Fairbanks climbed into cloud, and on emerging found himself almost over the airfield among more Fw 190s;

'I saw one going in to land but keep (sic) on going around the field & met another coming head on slightly below. I broke on to him and he pulled straight up for cloud. I stood on my tail too and fired from about 200 yds. & about 60° off – the E/A was almost stalled as I did so, & I saw him burst into flames at the wing root & the cockpit, the E/A rolled over slowly and went straight down. I saw the pilot bale out at about 500 ft. & the E/A went straight in and blew up.'

Two days later he was back again, catching and despatching a lone Fw 190 north of Plantlunne airfield. This was Fairbanks' final confirmed kill – his 13th (including one shared) – all but one flying the Tempest. It would seem that his victim was Feldwebel Erich Lange of III./JG 54, who was killed in his 'Dora 9' 'Black 13' (Wk-Nr 211095) at the time and location given in Fairbanks' combat report.

On the last day of February, Sqn Ldr Fairbanks led six of his Tempests to Hamm, Munster and Osnabruck early in the morning. A locomotive was attacked but then, shortly after 0800 hours, '40+ FW.190s and Me.109s' were seen north of Osnabruck. In typical fashion, Fairbanks led his flight into the attack, and a hard fight began, with little chance for the RAF pilots to get more than the odd shot in at their many opponents. Four Tempests returned, their pilots claiming dam-

No 501 Sqn, with whom Fairbanks claimed his first victory while flying a Spitfire. He is seated in the front row at the extreme left (*via A E Gunn*)

One of the Tempests flown by Fairbanks during his spell with No 3 Sqn was EJ777, which later flew with No 56 Sqn as 'US-F'. It is seen here in the latter markings at Volkel in February 1945 (*IWM FLM 3114*)

age to five Fw 190s, but two were missing, one of them flown by Fairbanks. It is now known that the combat was with the 'Dora 9s' of III./JG 26. Fairbanks and the other pilot, Flg Off Spence, both survived as PoWs, and after the war the former described the desperate action as follows;

'I called out a head-on attack and for the formation to drop long range tanks. Time was so short it was difficult to select a suitable target and lay-off deflection. I don't remember any return fire from the enemy aircraft. I think they were just as surprised as we were and also didn't have enough time to line up a burst. As soon as we passed the last man I called a left 180 degree break back toward the formation. As we turned around there were few aircraft to be seen. They must have scattered in all directions. I started to chase one that went into a cloud and I lost him. Shortly after this I pushed my aircraft down into cloud and came out underneath and saw a 190. By this time my No.2 had lost me.

'I closed the range on this aircraft and before I was ready to fire I noticed some tracers coming my way. I was near the ground and thought it was flak tracer. A few more tracers went by me and I was ready to fire at the enemy aircraft. I fired and hit the 190 who burst into flames. The next instant I was hit hard.

'It was not ground tracer I had seen but shells from the aircraft behind that hit me. I can remember seeing wing ribs and torn skin on the left and right upper wing surfaces and I was having difficulty keeping the aircraft level. The engine was missing and puffs of glycol were shooting by. No doubt my rad had been punctured. I held the stick hard over right to keep level and applied right rudder. With the controls in these positions I knew I wasn't going home. I decided it was time to bail out. Holding the controls with my right hand I tried to jettison the canopy with my left, but it wouldn't budge. I tried several times but didn't have enough strength in my left hand alone. I let go of the controls and pulled the jettison handle with both hands and away she went. I can only remember that the canopy was gone and that I leaned my head to the left into the slipstream. The next thing I remember I was on the ground.'

Immediately captured, Fairbanks was lucky not only to survive his brief parachute descent, but also the fate that befell a number of 2nd TAF pilots downed over Germany at this time – summary execution. It was a week before he reached the 'safety' of a PoW camp. Although his last kill was never officially claimed, it is apparently confirmed by Luftwaffe casualty records which show that Unteroffizier Franz Schmidt of 9./JG 26 was killed near Lengerich at 0810 hours flying Fw 190D-9 'white 17'.

While Fairbanks was in the PoW camp, a bar to his DFC was gazetted, followed by a second one just after the war when he was repatriated to Canada. However, unlike many wartime pilots, his flying career was not over. First resuming his education, he obtained an engineering degree from Cornell University, then while working for Sperry Gyroscopes, flew Vampires and T-33s with the RCAF Auxiliary. Two years were also spent in England, where he was able to fly Meteors with No 504 Sqn, RAuxAF. In 1955 he was employed by de Havilland Canada as a test pilot, flying Beavers, Otters and Caribou aircraft, and becoming an expert on STOL operations. After such a full aviation career, fraught with danger, it was an unexpected twist of fate when 'the Terror of Rheine' died of natural causes at the early age of 52.

Sqn Ldr David Fairbanks (right) with one of his No 274 Sqn flight commanders, Flt Lt 'Jesse' Hibbert, who would take over the unit when Fairbanks failed to return from a sortie on the last day of February 1945 (*IWM*)

APPENDICES - Appendix 1

Aces who flew Typhoons or Tempests but claimed less than five victories on those types
(*score includes some confirmed claims on these types)

		Units	Confirmed
F/O J A S Allen	Typhoon	56, 182	7
S/L J P Bartle	Typhoon	124 A/F	4/1
W/C E G Barwell	Tempest	FIU	9 1
W/C R P Beamont	Typhoon/Tempest	609, 150 Wg, 122 Wg	6/1*
S/L J Berry	Tempest	FIU, 501	3
W/C R P Brooker	Typhoon/Tempest	123 Wg, 122 Wg	7
S/L J R Cock	Tempest	3	10
W/C M N Crossley	Typhoon	Detling	20/2
W/C D Crowley-Milling	Typhoon	181, 121 Airfield	4/1
S/L E G Daniel	Typhoon/Tempest	1320 Flt, FIU	7
W/C R T P Davidson	Typhoon	175, 121 A/F, 143 Wg	4/2*
G/C B Drake	Typhoon	20 Wg	18/2
G/C H S L Dundas	Typhoon	56, Duxford	4/6
F/L W G Eagle	Typhoon	198	5*
W/C J F Edwards	Tempest	274	15/3
S/L R H Fokes	Typhoon	56, 257	9/4
S/L J A A Gibson	Tempest	80	12/1
G/C D E Gillam	Typhoon	Duxford, 146 Wg	7/1
W/C H C Godefroy	Typhoon	83 Gp HQ	7
F/L R A Haggar	Typhoon	56	7
G/C P P Hanks	Typhoon	56	13
F/L E W F Hewett	Typhoon	263	16
S/L W J Hibbert	Tempest	274	4/2*
F/L F W Higginson	Typhoon	56	12
F/L J A Houlton	Tempest	274	5/2*
S/L R J Hyde	Typhoon	197	5
W/C A Ingle	Typhoon	609	2/3
S/L W J Johnson	Typhoon	197, 257	4/3
F/L N G Jones	Tempest	FIU	6/1
W/C M T Judd	Typhoon	143 Wg, 121 Wg	4
S/L M P Kilburn	Tempest	56	6/1*
W/C J K Kilmartin	Typhoon	136 Wg	12/2
F/L G J King	Typhoon	609	6/1
S/L P W Lefevre	Typhoon	266	5/5
P/O H T Nicholls	Typhoon	137	6
G/C R P R Powell	Typhoon	121 Wg	7/2
W/C G L Raphael	Typhoon	Manston	7
W/C A C Rabagliati	Typhoon	Coltishall	16/1
W/C P H M Richey	Typhoon	609	10/1
S/L P R St Quintin	Tempest	56	9*
S/L G L Sinclair	Typhoon	1, 56	10
S/L R L Spurdle	Tempest	80	10
S/L B G Stapleton	Typhoon	257, 247	6/2
F/O B M Vassiliades	Tempest	3	8/2*
S/L J W Villa	Typhoon	198	13/4
S/L A D Wagner	Tempest	FIU	9
W/C D R Walker	Typhoon	175, 16 Wg, 124 Wg	4/1
S/L T Y Wallace	Typhoon	609	/1
W/C R C Wilkinson	Typhoon	1	7/2
F/L E L Williams	Tempest	FIU, 501	7
G/C H C A Woodhouse	Typhoon	16 Wg	3/2
G/C P G Wykeham-Barnes	Typhoon	257	14/3

Appendix 2

Typhoon and Tempest Aces

Pilot	Units	Confirmed Solo	Shared	Probables Solo	Shared	Damaged Solo	Shared	Aircraft	Confirmed (on other types)	Total confirmed
G/C J R Baldwin	609, 198, 146 Wg	15	1	1		4		Typhoon		15/1
S/L D C Fairbanks	274, 3	11	1	2				Tempest	1	12/1
W/C W E Schrader	486	9	2					Tempest	2	11/2
F/O C F J Detal	609	6	1					Typhoon		6/1
S/L R Van Lierde	609, 164, 3	6						Typhoon/Tempest		6
F/O J J Payton	56	6		1				Tempest		6
W/C E D Mackie	274, 80, 122 Wg	5	1			1		Tempest	15/2	20/3
S/L L W F Stark	609,263	5	1					Typhoon		5/1
F/O D E Ness	56	5	1					Tempest		5/1
S/L R A Lallemant	609, 198	5	1			1		Typhoon		5/1
S/L I J Sheddan	486	4	3					Tempest		4/3
S/L A E Umbers	486	4	1	1	1	2		Typhoon/Tempest		4/1
S/L K G Taylor-Cannon	486	4	1	1	1		1	Typhoon/Tempest		4/1
S/L J Niblett	198	4	1					Typhoon		4/1
S/L F Murphy	486	4		1				Typhoon		4
F/O A R Evans	486	4		1				Tempest		4
F/L P H Clostermann	274, 56, 3	4				2		Tempest	7	11
F/L I J Davies	609	4						Typhoon		4
F/O J Garland	80	4						Tempest		4
F/O V L Turner	56	4						Tempest		4
G/C J C Wells	609, 146 Wg	3	2			1		Typhoon		3/2
F/L A R Moore	3, 56	3	1		1			Tempest		3/1
W/C J M Bryan	198, 136 Wg	2	3			2		Typhoon	-/1	2/4
W/C J H Deall	266, 146 Wg	2	3					Typhoon		2/3
P/O H Shaw	56	2	3					Tempest		2/3
F/L J H Stafford	486	2	3					Typhoon		2/3
S/L P G Thornton-Brown	56, 609	2	3					Tempest		2/3
G/C D J Scott	486, 123 Wg	2	2	1		1		Typhoon		5/3
F/O N J Lucas	266	1	4			1	1	Typhoon		1/4

Appendix 3

Typhoon and Tempest V1 Aces

This appendix details pilots who shot down five or more V1 flying bombs while flying Typhoons or Tempests. Ranks given are the highest noted during research, and in most cases are those pertaining at the end of the war. Scores given include shared claims as whole numbers (number of shares given in brackets), and reflect recent research for *Aces High Volume 2*

	Unit	Confirmed		Unit	Confirmed
S/L J.Berry	FIU, 501	60 (1)	F/L F B Lawless	486	9
S/L R Van Lierde	3	44 (9)	F/O B F Miller	FIU, 501	9
W/C R P Beamont	150 Wing	31 (5)	F/L C B Thornton	FIU, 501	9
F/O R H Clapperton	3	24	F/O B M Hall	486	9 (3)
F/L A R Moore	3	24 (1)	F/O R D Bremner	486	9 (4)
F/S R W Cole	3	24 (4)	F/O R C Deleuze	501	8
F/L O D Eagleson	486	23 (3)	F/O W A Kalka	486	8
F/O R J Cammock	486	21 (1)	F/L J H Stafford	486	8
P/O H R Wingate	3	21 (2)	F/O K A Smith	486	8
F/L J H McCaw	486	20 (1)	S/L C J Sheddan	486	8 (1)
F/O K Slade-Betts	3	20 (1)	F/O W A Hart	486	8 (2)
S/L R Dryland	3	19 (2)	F/L W L Miller	486	7
S/L J R Cullen	486	18 (4)	F/O L G Everson	3	7 (1)
S/L A E Umbers	3	18 (4)	W/C H M Mason	486	7 (2)
P/O H J Bailey	3	14 (2)	P/O R W Pottinger	3	7 (3)
F/S D J MacKerras	3	14 (3)	F/L H Burton	501	6
F/L R J Robb	FIU, 501	13	F/O W A L Trott	486	6
F/O R E Barcklay	3	13 (1)	F/O W R MacLaren	56	6 (1)
F/O R J Danzey	486	13 (4)	F/S G H Wylde	56	6 (1)
P/O M J A Rose	3	12 (1)	F/L G L Bonham	501	5
F/O S B Feldman	3	12 (3)	S/L A S Dredge	3	5
F/L M F Edwards	3	12 (5)	S/L A R Hall	56	5
F/L E L Williams	FIU, 501	11	F/L D E Ness	56	5
S/L H N Sweetman	486	11 (1)	F/L N J Powell	486	5
F/O B J O'Connor	486	10 (1)	F/O S J Short	486	5
P/O H Shaw	56	10 (1)	F/O A N Sames	137	5
F/O G J M Hooper	486	10 (3)	F/L E W Tanner	486	5 (2)
F/L G K Whitman	3	10 (5)			

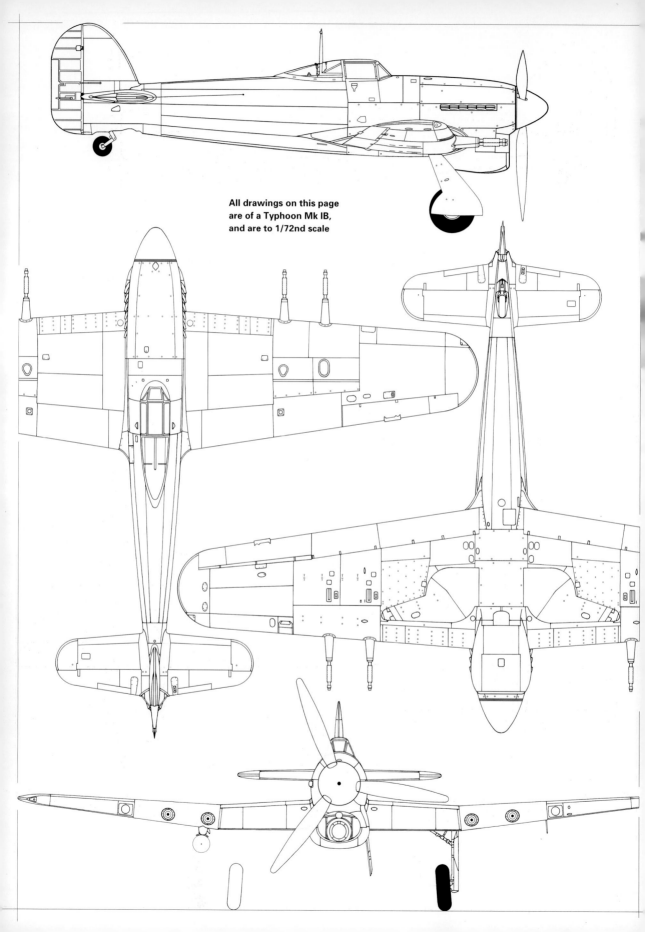

All drawings on this page
are of a Typhoon Mk IB,
and are to 1/72nd scale

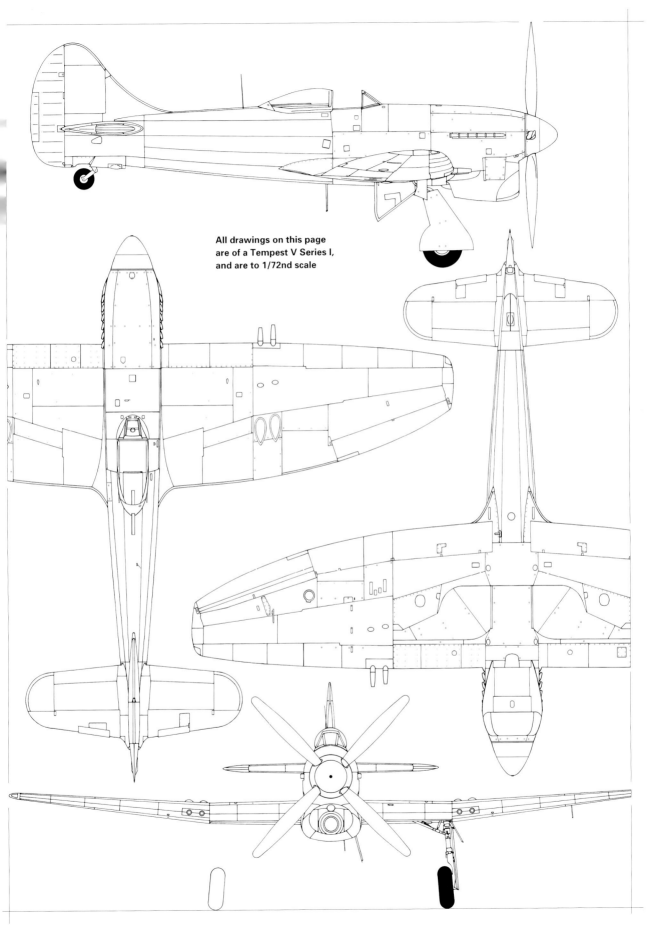

All drawings on this page
are of a Tempest V Series I,
and are to 1/72nd scale

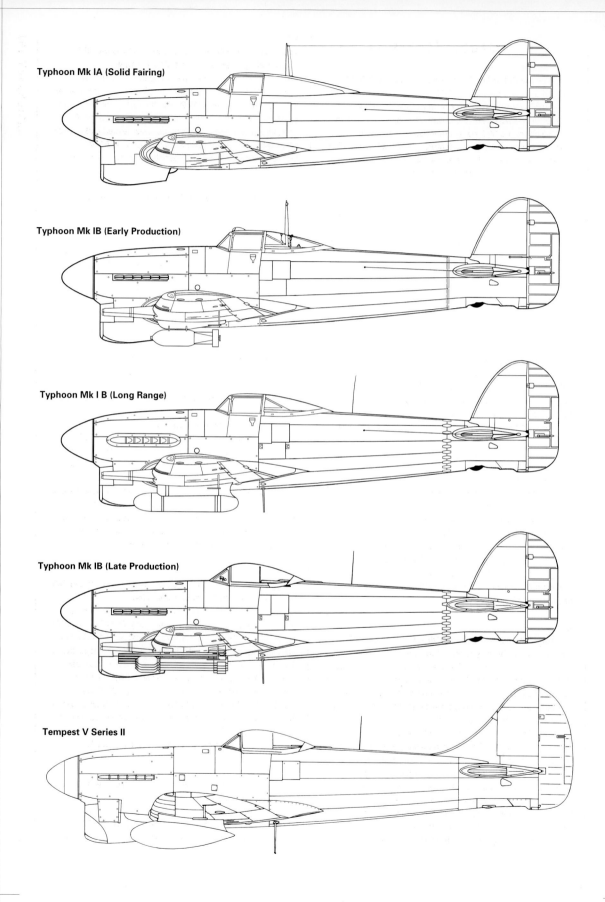

Typhoon Mk IA (Solid Fairing)

Typhoon Mk IB (Early Production)

Typhoon Mk I B (Long Range)

Typhoon Mk IB (Late Production)

Tempest V Series II

Colour Plates

1

Typhoon Mk IB R7698 of Wg Cdr D E Gillam, OC Duxford Wing, Duxford, September 1942

Delivered to No 609 Sqn in Mk IA form, R7698 was adopted by Gillam for his personal use and converted to Mk IB standard. The reason for the 'Z-Z' code rather than the expected 'DE-G' is not known, but it became a feature of his aircraft, adorning at least three more Typhoons and a Tempest. Note the over-sized fuselage roundel with rather odd proportions, caused by the modification of a 42-inch Type A1 roundel to C1 style (which should have been 36-inch diameter). The aircraft was repainted in a non-standard camouflage, and it has not been possible to determine the exact pattern owing to the use of apparently darker than normal grey. The Typhoon was marked with a 12-inch yellow band around each wing, centred on the inner cannon. When the Duxford Wing was disbanded, R7698 was allocated to the newly-formed No 198 Sqn, serving until July 1943 when it was retired to Taylorcraft, at Rearsby, for use in their Typhoon repair programme.

2

Typhoon Mk IB R8843 of Wg Cdr D J Scott, OC Tangmere Wing, Tangmere, September 1943

R8843 was the first Typhoon with a sliding hood to reach an operational unit, and was from a small batch of older Typhoons which had been in store awaiting adequate supplies of Sabre engines. These aircraft were brought up to the latest standard, and this included the fitting of the new canopy. The earliest 'bubble-tops' went to the COs of the Typhoon fighter squadrons, with another example being R8845, which was issued to Sqn Ldr Thornton-Brown of No 609 Sqn. Scott received his new Typhoon on 16 September 1943, and flew the aircraft until November, when he was posted to command RAF Hawkinge. Remaining at Tangmere, R8843 was damaged by flak while flown by Denys Gillam on 12 January 1944. Repaired by Taylorcraft, it was eventually issued to No 184 Sqn around D-Day. Transferred to No 175 Sqn a few days later, it was damaged and repaired again, whereupon it was issued to No 181 Sqn in September 1944. It was finally shot down by flak on 29 September 1944, with its pilot, Flt Lt T F Rosser, becoming a PoW.

3

Typhoon Mk IB MN570 of Wg Cdr R E P Brooker, OC No 123 Wing, Thorney Island, June 1944

Although issued to No 198 Sqn shortly before D-Day, MN570 was adopted by Wg Cdr Brooker for his personal use, carrying his single initial 'B', and flown by him until the end of his tour in July 1944. Spinner markings are based on the interpretation of black and white film, and should be regarded as provisional. Damaged in a landing accident by a No 198 Sqn pilot on the 24th of that month, MN570 was repaired and eventually reissued, first to No 247 Sqn (as 'ZY-F') in November 1944, and then to No 174 Sqn the following month, becoming 'XP-P'. Its fate is obscure, but there is evidence to suggest it was written off in a crash landing at Volkel after being hit by flak on 22 February 1945. Brooker later flew Tempest NV641, which also coded 'B', from January 1945. and was posted missing while flying this aircraft on 16 April 1945.

4

Typhoon Mk IB SW470 of Grp Capt J R Baldwin, OC No 123 Wing, Plantlunne (B.103), May 1945

When Johnny Baldwin returned to operations at the end of February 1945, he again adopted two Typhoons, both marked 'JB' – the bomber was SW496 and the rocket-armed aircraft was SW470, which he retained for four months after VE-Day. The spinner was originally black, but was painted pink(!) circa May 1945. By January 1946 SW470 was at No 51 MU at Lichfield, and was scrapped there the following September.

5

Typhoon Mk IB MN518 of Wg Cdr R T P Davidson, OC No 143 Wing, Hurn, May 1944

Davidson received MN518 late in April 1944 as a replacement for his earlier 'R-D' (see JP496/Profile 10), and flew it on operations during early May. On 8 May, however, while leading No 438 Sqn in an attack on a 'Noball' site near Douai in a borrowed aircraft (MM957 'F3-N'), he was forced to land in France with engine failure. He evaded capture and fought with the *Maquis* until liberated. MN518 was taken over by the new Wing Commander Flying, M T Judd, and was recoded 'MJ'. Damaged on D-Day +1, it was repaired and issued to No 266 Sqn as 'ZH-C' in September. It survived the war to be scrapped at No 5 MU at Kemble in July 1946.

6

Typhoon Mk IB MN587 of Grp Capt D E Gillam, OC No 146 Wing, Antwerp (B.70), October 1944

Although marked 'ZZ II', MN587 was Denys Gillam's third (at least) Typhoon to carry 'ZZ' codes. Allocated to No 266 Sqn, it was flown by Gillam during his time as Commanding Officer of No 146 Wing between July and December 1944. He led many strikes in this aircraft, despite his role, strictly speaking, being non-operational. Following damage to the tailwheel unit on 26 December 1944 while being flown by another pilot, MN587 was withdrawn for repair and subsequently flew with No 84 Group Support Unit as a training machine. It was scrapped at No 5 MU, Kemble, in October 1946.

7

Typhoon Mk IB PD521 of Wg Cdr J R Baldwin, OC No 146 Wing, Antwerp (B.70), November 1944

Johnny Baldwin few several Typhoons marked with his initials, the first as Wing Commander Flying No 146 Wing on 22 June 1944. When the Wing moved to France in July he flew 'JB I' and 'JB II', equipped for bombs and rockets respectively. The latter was MN934 until 13 August, when it was crash-landed following flak damage – the serial of its next two replacements are not known, but the fourth 'JB II' was PD521, flown between 30 September and 11 October, when Baldwin was posted 'on rest'. PD521 went on to serve with Nos 257 and 266 Sqns, finishing the war with the latter unit as 'ZH-Z'. It was scrapped at No 51 MU in August 1946.

8

Typhoon Mk IA R7648 of Sqn Ldr H S L Dundas, OC No 56 Sqn, Duxford, June 1942

This Typhoon was the fourth of Dundas' personal aircraft to carry the name *'Farquhar'*. It was delivered to No 56 Sqn in early April 1942, replacing the previous 'A', R7593. Dundas flew this Typhoon on the first defensive patrols whilst commanding a detachment at Westhampnett in June 1942. R7648 was replaced the following month by Typhoon Mk IB R7825. Promoted to lead the Typhoon fighter-bomber Wing forming at Duxford in late 1942, Dundas briefly flew a Typhoon with the personal code 'H-D', which is believed to have been R7684. This aircraft had previously served as the station commander's aircraft (coded 'JG' for John Grandy).

9
Typhoon Mk IB MN134 of Flg Off A N Sames, No 137 Sqn, Manston, June 1944

Originally coded 'SF-N' when it joined No 137 Sqn on 3 March 1944, MN134 was recoded 'SF-S' by May. During June and July it became No 137 Sqn's top V1 hunter, with nine destroyed by its pilots. Flg Off 'Arty' Sames, the only Typhoon V1 ace, used this aircraft to claim three of his five kills, and Wg Cdr Raphael (OC Manston), also claimed one in this aircraft on the night of 6/7 July 1944. MN134 continued in service with No 137 Sqn until the last day of 1944 when it was damaged, and eventually returned to the UK for repair at Taylorcraft of Rearsby. It saw no further active service and was scrapped at No 5 MU at Kemble in October 1946.

10
Typhoon Mk IB JP496 of Sqn Ldr R T P Davidson, OC No 175 Sqn, Lydd, August 1943

Allocated to No 175 Sqn on 12 July 1943, JP496 was coded 'HH-W' and adopted by Sqn Ldr Davidson. It displayed his pennant and five kill markings – two Japanese, two Italian and one German. When promoted to Wing Commander Flying No 121 Wing, he kept this Typhoon, which was repainted with his abbreviated initials 'R-D', and had the appropriate pennant applied. Davidson took this aircraft with him when posted to lead No 143 (RCAF) Wing. When replaced by MN518, JP596 went to Cunliffe Owen for canopy and RP modifications, and was then delivered to No 3 Tactical Exercise Unit on 10 June 1944. It later served with No 56 OTU and was scrapped at No 5 MU at Kemble in September 1946.

11
Typhoon Mk IB EK270 of Sqn Ldr D Crowley-Milling, OC No 181 Sqn, Appledram, June 1943

EK270, marked with the unofficial squadron badge of the period, was flown by Crowley-Milling on dive-bomber sorties over Northern France between May and August 1943. When he was promoted to lead No 121 Wing, it was returned to Hawkers for repairs and emerged with a sliding hood and RP equipment to become 'SF-H' of No 137 Sqn in the following March. After 11 months with the latter unit it was damaged, and after repair was issued to No 247 Sqn as 'ZY-E'. Damaged just ten days after its returne to action, the Typhoon was shipped back to the UK for repair by Marshall of Cambridge, but was scrapped there in May 1945.

12
Typhoon Mk IB EK195 of Plt Off J A S Allen, No 182 Sqn, Appledram, June 1943

Delivered to No 182 Sqn on 5 June 1943, EK195 had a short operational career. On the 21st of the same month, Plt Off 'Sandy' Allen was badly hit by flak near Les Hayons, but man-

aged to return safely despite large holes in the fin and rudder. The aircraft was despatched to No 13 MU at Henlow, but there is no further record of its use. It is likely that it was reduced to spares for use in the rebuild programme – the fate of many damaged Typhoons at this time. On 30 June Allen was hit by flak over France again while flying JP381 'XM-C' and badly wounded. He did not return to operational flying.

13
Typhoon Mk IB EK273 of Sqn Ldr Don 'Butch' Taylor, OC No 195 Sqn, Ludham, June 1943

Most unusually for a squadron commander's aircraft, EK273 carries Taylor's initials in place of a squadron letter. 'Butch' Taylor had flown with No 64 Sqn during the Battle of Britain, claiming a share in a Do 217 destroyed and a Bf 110. When No 195 Sqn was disbanded in the reorganisation of the 2nd TAF, he took command of No 197 Sqn, completing his tour in July 1944. Taylor returned to commence a final tour, again on Typhoons, with No 193 Sqn in April 1945. On 6 July 1943 he flew to Ludham's parent station, Coltishall, and lent his EK273 to the Wing Commander Flying, A C Rabagliati, who then led No 56 Sqn on a shipping strike from which he failed to return.

14
Typhoon Mk IB MM987 of Sqn Ldr J R Baldwin, OC No 198 Sqn, Manston, March 1944

When Johnny Baldwin took command of No 198 Sqn at the end of November 1943, he inherited Sqn Ldr Mike Bryan's Typhoon, 'TP-X'. He soon adopted 'TP-Z' as his aircraft, but on 19 December he tested a new 'Z', which he described in his log as 'my new sliding hood job' – this is believed to have been R8894. He flew this aircraft until the end of January 1944, when he went to Milfield to attend the Fighter Leader School. R8894 was lost in action on 10 February 1944 while being flown by Wt Off Stanley (PoW), and its replacement may well have been MM987, which arrived on the squadron the next day. The tentative identification of 'TP-Z', which figured in a series of publicity photos taken at the beginning of March 1944, as MM987 is reinforced by the fact that Baldwin last flew 'TP-Z' on 4 March in a practice for an attack on a radar site, and MM987 was damaged in an accident that same day (while flown by another pilot).

15
Typhoon Mk IB MP126 of Sqn Ldr B G Stapleton, OC No 247 Sqn, Eindhoven (B.78), December 1944

MP126 was allocated to No 247 Sqn on the last day of August 1944 and was adopted by Battle of Britain ace 'Gerrie' Stapleton, who had taken command of the unit earlier in the month. In October No 247 Sqn Typhoons were treated to a spate of adornment, and MP126 gained the artwork shown, executed by squadron Intelligence Officer, Flg Off Kay. Serviceable Typhoons were always in short supply in 2nd TAF, and on 5 December 'ZY-Y' was 'borrowed' by Dutch pilot Plt Off Fricky Wiersum, who was downed by flak near Rhede. He managed to make a forced landing behind the lines, where his captors showed great interest in the artwork!

16
Typhoon Mk IB JP510 of Sqn Ldr R H Fokes, OC No 257 Sqn, Warmwell, August 1943

Battle of Britain ace 'Ronnie' Fokes took command of No 257 Sqn in July 1943, where he flew JP510,which carried a rank pennant and a name, believed to be *'Cowboy II'*. He flew this Typhoon until 14 January 1944, when it went to Hawkers for canopy modifications. It returned to No 257 Sqn on 2 March as 'FM-Y' and was lost on a 'Noball' attack two weeks later. Fokes' new 'A' was MN118, replaced in turn during April by MN372 – he was killed in action flying the latter on D+6.

17

Typhoon Mk IB JP846 of Sqn Ldr P W Lefevre, OC No 266 Sqn, Harrowbeer, January 1944

Battle of Britain and Malta ace Peter Lefevre took over No 266 Sqn in August 1943. JP846 became his aircraft when it was delivered to the unit on 25 September. It was coded 'ZH-G' following a precedent set by the first Typhoon CO, Charles Green. Lefevre claimed a share in a Ju 88 on 1 December, a Bf 109 on 21 January 1944 and a share in a Fw 190 two days later, all while flying JP846. He was killed when he bailed out too low after JP846 had been hit by flak attacking coastal defences at Aber-Wrach, in Brittany, on 6 February 1944.

18

Typhoon Mk IB JP906 of Flg Off N J Lucas, No 266 Sqn, Harrowbeer, October 1943

Delivered to No 266 Sqn just four days after JP846 above, JP906 was coded 'ZH-L'. On 15 October 1943, Flg Off N J Lucas pursued two Fw 190s in this aircraft, along with his No 2, Sgt Drummond. Both enemy aircraft were downed, with one and one shared credited to Lucas. This Typhoon saw further action on 1 December 1943 when it was flown by Flg Off S J P Blackwell on a 'Ranger' to southern Brittany, the pilot despatching a minesweeping Ju 52 near Isle de Groix, before attacking a Ju 88. He was then hit by return fire and went down (surviving and evading), leaving the Ju 88 to three other No 266 Sqn pilots – Blackwell was awarded a quarter-share.

19

Typhoon Mk IB RB281 of Flg Off A H Fraser, No 439 Sqn, Eindhoven (B.78), February 1945

This late production Typhoon was allocated to No 439 Sqn RCAF on 28 December 1944. Just four days later, in the aftermath of the infamous Luftwaffe New Year's Day attack on Allied airfields, Flg Off Hugh Fraser piloted this aircraft in a low-level dogfight with a large number of Fw 190s. Fraser destroyed two, the second one being a 'Dora'. In a further combat in this aircraft, on 14 February, he destroyed a Me 262 of 5./KG(J) 51. Returning from an operation on 2 March, RB281 suffered an engine failure and Fraser crash-landed near Eindhoven. The aircraft was repaired by Taylorcraft at Rearsby, but went into store at No 5 MU at Kemble, only to be scrapped there in November 1946.

20

Typhoon Mk IB R8781 of Sgt K G Taylor-Cannon, No 486 Sqn, Tangmere, December 1942

R8781 is shown wearing the short-lived white nose identification markings and underwing black stripes which were prescribed for Typhoons in November 1942. Orders for the removal of the white nose markings, and addition of white stripes between the black, were issued on 5 December, but removal from the whole squadron would have taken several days, so it is possible that they were still displayed when Flg Off G G Thomas destroyed a Bf 109 of 4(F)/123 on Christmas Eve 1942. Sgt 'Hyphen' Taylor-Cannon claimed a Bf 109 in this aircraft on 17 January 1943, and it shared in the destruction of another Bf 109 on 14 April 1943 when flown by Flt Sgt R H Fitzgibbon. After service with Nos 195 and 164 Sqns, R8781 spent most of 1944 and early 1945 in repair units, before finally being issued to No 266 Sqn in Germany postwar. It was scrapped at No 51 MU in September 1946.

21

Typhoon Mk IB EJ981 of Sqn Ldr D J Scott, OC No 486 Sqn, Tangmere, June 1943

Scott flew EJ981 'SA-F' on many operations between 12 June and 2 September 1943. He claimed two Fw 190s while flying this aircraft, one on 24 June and the other, shared with Plt Off Fitzgibbon, on 15 July. Re-coded 'SA-E' in September, it was written off following a forced landing due to engine failure on 20 November 1943 while flown by Flt Sgt Helean.

22

Typhoon Mk IB R7752 of Sqn Ldr R P Beamont, OC No 609 Sqn, Manston, February 1943

Delivered to No 609 Sqn on 2 June 1942, R7752 was coded 'PR-G' and flown by Sqn Ldr Paul Richey (he had flown Hurricane 'JX-G' in the battle of France). When 'Bee' Beamont took over command in October 1942, he also inherited 'G', personalising the aircraft with a yellow spinner and cannon fairings, and his scoreboard. It also had a broad yellow band beneath the radiator fairing and 12-inch wide yellow stripes on the upper wing surfaces in line with the inner cannon – these were removed on 3 February 1943. 'Tally ho' was No 609 Sqn's motto. Although wreaking havoc on enemy rail stock on night intruders, air combat eluded 'Bee' and 'G', except for the night of 18 January 1943 when he was able to damage a Ju 88. R7752 was eventually taken over by No 56 Sqn in July 1943, but the following month it was delivered to Hawker Aircraft and reduced to components.

23

Typhoon Mk IB R7855 of Flg Off R A Lallemant, No 609 Sqn, Manston, February 1943

One of the most successful Typhoons in air combat, R7855 was allocated to 'Cheval' Lallemant. Together, they were responsible for the destruction of four Fw 190s,on 19 December 1942, 20 January 1943 and 14 February 1943 (two), and probably a fifth on the latter date. The Typhoon had yellow wing bands for the same period as R7752 above. Following combat damage on 16 April 1943, R7855 was returned to Hawker Aircraft for repair, but was reassessed and dismantled for components at the end of June. Lallemant increased his score on his second tour, with No 198 Sqn.

24

Typhoon Mk IB SW411 of Sqn Ldr L W F Stark, OC No 609 Sqn, Plantlunne (B.103), May 1945

When 'Pinkie' Stark returned to No 609 Sqn for his second tour, it was as Commanding Officer. He retained SW411 as his personal aircraft from 19 March 1945 until the unit was disbanded the following September. The gloss black and yellow spinner scheme was applied a few days after VE-Day. The inner surfaces of the undercarriage doors were also yellow with white edging. Stored at No 5 MU at Kemble for a year, SW411 was finally scrapped in October 1946.

25
Tempest Mk V EJ750 of Wg Cdr Wray, OC No 122 Wing, Volkel (B.80), November 1944

Allocated to No 486 Sqn on 19 October 1944, EJ750 was in fact used by the Wing Commander Flying No 122 Wing, and carried his initials 'JBW'. John Wray made two aerial claims while flying this aircraft – both Me 262s – on 3 November and 17 December 1944. When Wray was replaced by Wg Cdr Brooker in January 1945, EJ750 was recoded 'SA-B' and flown by No 486 Sqn pilots, who made claims on 1 January 1945 (Plt Off Hooper, Bf 109 destroyed), and 23 January 1945 (Flt Lt Miller, FW 190 damaged, and Wt Off Bailey, Bf109 shared destroyed). EJ750 was struck by debris during a shipping attack on 8 February 1945 and force-landed in enemy territory, its pilot, Flt Lt Miller, evading capture.

26
Tempest Mk V SN228 of Wg Cdr E D Mackie, OC No 122 Wing, Fassberg (B.152), May 1945

Promoted to command No 122 Wing at the end of April 1945, Mackie picked brand new Tempest SN228 to carry his initials, flying it into action for the first time on 3 May. Shown here in its wartime markings, SN228 later carried a 25-kill tally immediately in front of the pennant, No 122 Wing's official badge on the fin tip, and its spinner repainted in a lighter (unknown) colour. Last flown by Mackie on 12 October 1945, the aircraft was allocated to No 41 Sqn the following week. The unit was soon renumbered No 26 Sqn, and wearing codes 'XC-D', SN228 became the mount of Sqn Ldr H Ambrose. After transfer to No 33 Sqn in September 1946, it was put into store at No 5 MU at Kemble in October 1946, before being sold for scrap to J Dale in November 1950.

27
Tempest Mk V JN751 of Wg Cdr R P Beamont, OC No 150 Wing, Newchurch, June 1944

One of the first Tempests in operational service, JN751 was allocated to No 3 Sqn on 16 March 1944, but was adopted by the Wing Commander Flying, No 150 Wing, R P Beamont, as his personal mount. It carried his initials, and rank pennant (facing the wrong direction for a flag!), and sported a yellow spinner similar to that on his No 609 Sqn Typhoon. Shortly before D-Day it was marked with smarter than usual 'invasion stripes', as they were factory-applied by Hawker at Langley. Beamont made the first Tempest air-to-air claim while flying this aircraft over Rouen on D+2, and scored the majority of his 31 'Diver' claims in this aircraft. JN751 was replaced in early in September 1944 by a new Series 2 Tempest Mk V, coded 'RPB' (serial not known). Refurbished at Langley, JN751 was returned to service in December 1944 with anti-aircraft co-operation unit, No 287 Sqn. It crashed on the Isle of Sheppey in bad visibility, killing its pilot, on 18 May 1945.

28
Tempest Mk V JN862 of Flt Lt R Van Lierde, No 3 Sqn, Newchurch, June 1944

'Mony' Van Lierde followed a very successful tour on Typhoons with a posting to No 3 Sqn as a flight commander, flying Tempests. In the summer of 1944 he became the most successful pilot, by day, against V1 flying bombs, claiming 44 destroyed. Most of his claims were made while flying his personal aircraft, JN862. A close study of the well known photo of this aircraft reveals three narrow bands at the tip of the spinner – these are believed to have been the Belgian national colours. The fighter was replaced in August 1944 by EJ557 when JN862's undercarriage collapsed on landing. After repair it became 'JF-Q', but was damaged again on 17 September 1944 when a long-range tank fell of while landing. Repaired again, it was stored at No 20 MU and eventually sold to Hawkers in November 1950 (presumably for spares retrieval).

29
Tempest Mk V NV994 of Flt Lt P H Clostermann, No 3 Sqn, Hopsten (B.112), April 1945

Delivered to No 3 Sqn on 15 April 1945, NV994 was coded 'JF-E' and frequently flown by 'A' Flight commander, Flt Lt Pierre Clostermann. On 20 April he destroyed two Fw 190s in one sortie in this aircraft – later claims were made in SN222, code letter not known. NV994 was declared 'Cat B' on 1 July 1945 (cause not known) and repaired by Hawker Aircraft at Langley. It was then stored at No 20 MU at Aston Down until April 1950, when it was returned to Hawker Aircraft for conversion to TT 5 (target-tug) standard. Issued in April 1952 to Sylt Armament Practice Station (APS) it served as 'D' until October 1954, when it went into store at No 20 MU again, before finally being sold back to the manufacturers in July 1955.

30
Tempest Mk V EJ880 of Flt Lt L C Luckhoff, No 33 Sqn, Gilze-Rijen (B.77), February 1945

Delivered to No 33 Sqn in December 1944, EJ880 was flown by Flt Lt Luckhoff in a combat with Bf 109s of I./JG 27 on 25 February 1945, during which Luckhoff was credited with the destruction of two of the enemy aircraft. He was also hit by flak on the same sortie, but returned safely to base. EJ880 was returned to Hawker Aircraft for repair; and on completion in December 1946, it was stored at No 5 MU at Kemble until returned again to Hawkers for conversion to target towing. It served with APS Sylt from April 1952 until October 1954, when it went into store at No 20 MU at Aston Down, before finally being sold back to the manufacturers in July 1955.

31
Tempest Mk V EJ578 of Flg Off J J Payton, No 56 Sqn, Grimbergen (B.60), September 1944

Jim Payton, one of the most successful Tempest pilots in air combat, usually flew 'US-I'. The first so marked was EJ546, which was soon damaged by a V1 explosion – its replacement was EJ578, in which Payton made his first claim, a Fw 190 'probable' on 29 September 1944. Wg Cdr Beamont borrowed the aircraft on 2 October 1944, when he made his last air combat claim before becoming a PoW ten days later. EJ578 was transferred to No 419 Repair and Salvage Unit on 31 October, and was issued to No 274 Sqn on 11 November. Damaged on 14 January 1945, when its undercarriage collapsed on landing, it spent the rest of its life either under repair or in storage, before being repurchased by Hawkers in November 1950.

32

Tempest Mk V EJ667 of Flg Off J W Garland, No 80 Sqn, Volkel (B.80), December 1944

EJ667 was normally flown by Flg Off John 'Judy' Garland, who claimed a Me 262 destroyed on 2 December 1944, a Fw 190 on 27 December 1944 (in EJ667) and two Fw 190s on 1 January 1945. It later flew with No 3 Sqn, and was eventually converted to TT 5 standard in 1950. Given a second of life in this role, EJ667 target towed with the Central Gunnery School at Leconfield (as 'FJU-M') and at APS Sylt (as 'K'). It was re-purchased by Hawkers in July 1955.

33

Tempest Mk V NV700 of Sqn Ldr E D Mackie, OC No 80 Sqn, Volkel (B.80), March 1945

On taking command of No 80 Sqn in January 1945, 'Rosie' Mackie flew NV657, but when this was damaged on 2 February 1945, he replaced it with NV700, which had pre-viously seen service with No 56 OTU. He added the last three of his solo claims to his impressive score in this aircraft on 7 March (Fw 190D) and 9 April 1945 (two Ar 96s). Damaged later in the month, it was replaced by SN189. After repair and storage, NV700 was sold to Hawkers in November 1950.

34

Tempest Mk V NV774 of Flt Lt L McAuliffe, No 222 Sqn, Gilze-Rijen (B.77), March 1945

Responsible for one of only three Ar 234s shot down by Tempests, NV774 had been delivered to No 222 Sqn on 8 February 1945, and served with that unit until the Tempests were left at Weston Zoyland on 23 October 1945 while the pilots proceeded to Molesworth for re-equipment with Meteors. On 14 March 1945, No 222 Sqn was credited with the destruction of an Ar 234 from KG 76 which had attacked Remagen Bridge – it was shared by Flt Lt McAuliffe in NV774 and Flg Off McClelland in NV670 'ZD-X'. From Weston Zoyland, NV774 was allocated to No 16 School of Technical Training, and was eventually scrapped there in May 1947.

35

Tempest Mk V EJ762 of Flt Lt D C Fairbanks, No 274 Sqn, Volkel (B.80), November 1945

Allocated to No 274 Sqn on 28 September 1944, EJ762 was first flown on operations by Fairbanks on 17 October, and it remained his favoured mount until 19 November when it was badly damaged by flak. Once repaired, EJ762 was flown by Fairbanks just once more, on 17 December, and he claimed two Bf 109s destroyed and a third damaged during the sortie. He was then posted to No 3 Sqn as a flight commander. EJ762 force-landed in enemy territory in 1 February 1945, its pilot, Flt Lt G J Bruce, becoming a PoW.

36

Tempest Mk V NV722 of Sqn Ldr W J Hibbert, OC No 274 Sqn, Volkel (B.80), March 1945

Although 'Jesse' Hibbert made no air combat claims while fly-ing this aircraft, it was his favoured mount while commanding No 274 Sqn in March 1945. Flt Lt Pierre Clostermann also flew it on at least two occasions during his spell with No 274 Sqn. After damage in April, it was repaired by No 151 Repair Unit and issued to No 486 Sqn on 1 May 1945 as 'SA-Q'. The

very next day it fell to flak near Lubeck, its pilot, Flg Off Owen Eagleson (No 486 Sqn's top V1 'killer'), evading capture.

37

Tempest Mk V JN803 of Wt Off J H Stafford, No 486 Sqn, Grimbergen (B.60), September 1944

Arriving on No 486 Sqn on 17 May 1944, JN803 became one of the top V1 'killing' Tempests. Its scoreboard indicates 26 kills, which it is believed were applicable to the aircraft rather than any one pilot – no less than 13 made claims flying this aircraft, with both Plt Off Stafford and Wt Off Kalka getting four V1s apiece in JN803. Following repairs in November, it was issued to No 3 Sqn on 7 December 1944 and lost, with its pilot, 23 days later when downed by a Bf 109 from JG 27.

38

Tempest Mk V SN129 of Sqn Ldr C J Sheddan, OC No 486 Sqn, Fassberg (B.152), May 1945

SN129 carries the pennant and scoreboard of Jimmy Sheddan, No 486 Sqn's last wartime CO. The aircraft was allocated to the unit on 13 March 1945, and its first combat success came on 10 April when 'Smokey' Schrader claimed a Fw 190. Jack Stafford got another Fw 190 on 12 April and Sheddan a third on the 14th. The next day SN129 was again successful against Fw 190s, Brian O'Connor claiming one destroyed and another damaged – the latter was assessed as destroyed and shared with Sqn Ldr Mackie and another No 80 Sqn pilot. Sheddan shared in the destruction of yet another on 16 April, and celebrated his promotion to command the unit on 2 May with a final (shared) claim for an unidentified four-engined flying boat. When No 486 Sqn disbanded in September 1945, its Tempests were handed over to No 41 Sqn which, on 1 April 1946, was re-numbered No 26 Sqn. By 26 April 1946 SN129 was in store at No 20 MU at Aston Down, and was sold to Hawkers in November 1950.

39

Tempest Mk V NV969 of Sqn Ldr W E Schrader, OC No 486 Sqn, Hopsten (B.112), April 1945

Flown by 'Smokey' Schrader during most of his run of successes, NV969 had arrived on No 486 Sqn at the end of March 1945. First claim for the partnership came on 15 April (two FW 190s), with further victories coming thick and fast – Fw 190s on 16 and 29 April, Bf 109s on 21and (two and a shared) 29 April. No postwar fate of storage and scrapping awaited NV969, for on 19 June 1945 it shed wing panels dur-ing a formation flight and plunged into the sea off Copenhagen – pilot Owen Eagleson escaped by parachute.

40

Tempest Mk V EJ558 of Flg Off B F Miller (USAAF), No 501 Sqn, Bradwell Bay, October 1944

Replacing EJ538, EJ558 arrived on No 501 Sqn on 31 August 1944. Often flown by Flg Off 'Bud' Miller (a USAAF exchange pilot), it carried his 'Diver' scoreboard in front of the cockpit. Miller claimed his last V1, in this aircraft, on the night of 24/25 September 1944. Subsequently, Flg Off J A L Johnson claimed two in EJ558 on the night of 21/22 October 1944. On 20 February 1945 it was damaged by debris from a ground target while testing the cannons, and after repair, it was stored at No 20 MU until sold to Hawkers in November 1950.

FIGURE PLATES

1

During the Normandy campaign 2nd TAF pilots were issued with army battledress, which was meant to help their identification as Allied personnel if downed in a battle area. Sqn Ldr A E Umbers, CO of No 486 Sqn, RNZAF, is seen here still wearing this issue in early 1945, along with a side-arm. He is also wearing 1942 Issue flying boots, which were preferred by some pilots, and were perhaps warmer during the winter of 1944/45, and a forage cap (popular in 2nd TAF).

2

Wg Cdr R P Beamont, Wing Commander Flying No 150 Wing, wears standard RAF battledress with 'escape boots' which, if necessary, could be cut down to resemble civilian shoes to aid evasion. The right boot has a dagger riveted to the side, for use in emergencies involving tangled webbing, or to puncture a dinghy accidentally inflated in the cockpit.

3

Wg Cdr D J Scott, RNZAF, Tangmere Wing Leader in late 1943, went on to become the youngest group captain (at 26) in the RNZAF. His companion is a wire-haired terrier called 'Kim' (with the Kennel Club name of 'Napier Sabre'!), who had been presented by Turton and Platts, manufacturers of the Sabre's sleeve valves.

4

Flg Off Hugh Fraser, a Typhoon fighter-bomber pilot of No 439 Sqn, RCAF, is also wearing army battledress and 'escape boots'. Despite completing 68 operational sorties towards the end of the war, and shooting down three enemy aircraft (including a rare Me 262 victory), he failed to receive any award. A full tour of operations was usually 95 to 120 sorties for 2nd TAF Typhoon pilots.

5

Sqn Ldr Johnny Baldwin, Typhoon top-scorer, is seen here as CO of No 198 Sqn in the winter of 1943/44. He also went on to become a group captain at the age of 26. Baldwin is wearing a monogrammed Mae-West and his trousers cover his 'escape boots'.

6

Sqn Ldr David Fairbanks, RCAF (although a US citizen), was the CO of No 274 Sqn in February 1945. The top-scoring Tempest pilot of the war, he is seen wearing standard RAF battledress and old pattern flying boots beneath his trouser legs. Perhaps, as CO he felt he had to set an example to his men, for pilots' attire in 2nd TAF frontline units tended to be rather more casual than this in the final months of conflict in Europe, as several of these uniform profiles attest to!

BIBLIOGRAPHY

AVERY, MAX & SHORES, CHRISTOPHER, *Spitfire Leader*. Grub Street, 1997

BASHOW, DAVID L. Lt Col, *All the Fine Young Eagles*. Stoddart, 1997

BEAMONT, R.P. CBE, DSO & bar, DFC & Bar, Wg Cdr, *Tempests Over Europe*. Airlife, 1994

BEAMONT, R.P. CBE, DSO & bar, DFC & Bar, Wg Cdr, *Fighter Test Pilot*. PSL, 1986

BEAMONT, R.P. CBE, DSO & bar, DFC & Bar, Wg Cdr, *My Part of the Sky*. PSL, 1989

CALDWELL, DONALD, *The JG 26 War Diary Volume Two*. Grub Street, 1998

DUNDAS, HUGH, *Flying Start*. Stanley Paul, 1988

FLANAGAN, MIKE, *Typhoon Types*. Newton, 1997

FRANKS, NORMAN, *The Battle of the Airfields*. Grub Street, 1995

FRANKS, NORMAN, *The Greatest Air Battle*. William Kimber, 1979

FRANKS, NORMAN, *Typhoon Attack*. William Kimber, 1984

FRANKS, NORMAN & RICHEY, PAUL. DFC, *Fighter Pilot's Summer*. Grub Street, 1993

HALLIDAY, HUGH. A., *Typhoon and Tempest, the Canadian Story*. CANAV Books, 1992

LALLEMAN R. DFC, Lt Col, *Rendezvous With Fate*. Macdonald, 1964

SHEDDAN C. J. DFC, Sqn Ldr with FRANKS, NORMAN, *Tempest Pilot*. Grub Street, 1993

SHORES, CHRISTOPHER, *2nd Tactical Air Force*. Osprey, 1970

SHORES, CHRISTOPHER & WILLIAMS, CLIVE, *Aces High*. Grub Street, 1994

SCOTT D. J. DSO, OBE, DFC & bar, Grp Capt, *Typhoon Pilot*. Leo Cooper, 1982

SCOTT D. J. DSO, OBE, DFC & bar, Grp Capt, *One More Hour*. Hutchinson, 1989

SORTEHAUG, PAUL, *The Wild Winds*. Paul Sortehaug, 1998

SPURDLE, BOB, DFC & bar, Sqn Ldr, *The Blue Arena*. William Kimber, 1986

SWEETING, DENIS, DFC, *Wings of Chance*. ABP, 1990

THOMAS, CHRIS & SHORES, CHRISTOPHER, *The Typhoon and Tempest Story*. Arms & Armour, 1988

ZIEGLER, FRANK, *The Story of 609 Sqn*. Macdonald, 1971

Wing Operations Record Books	Air 26, PRO
Squadron Operations Record Books	Air 27, PRO
Combat Reports	Air 50, PRO
Fighter Command Losses and Claims	Air 16/961 & 962, PRO
2nd TAF Losses and Claims	Air 37/5, 6 & 7, PRO